PUBLIC
MANAGEMENT
A Case Handbook

PUBLIC
MANAGEMENT
A Case Handbook

Publisher | Kim Jun-young
Printed by | Sungkyunkwan University Press
First Published 2014. 8

Authors | Sung Min Park, Seona Kim
Production Editor | Shin Chul-ho
Designer | Chorokbanana

Sungkyunkwan University Press
25-2 Sungkyunkwan-ro, Jongno-gu
Seoul 110-745, Korea
Tel | 82-2-760-1253~4, Fax: 82-2-762-7452
http://press.skku.edu

ISBN 979-11-5550-066-8 93350

This work was supported by the National Research Foundation of Korea Grant funded by the Korean
Government (NRF-2013S1A3A2055042).

PUBLIC
MANAGEMENT

A Case Handbook

Sung Min Park & Seona Kim

Sungkyunkwan University Press

About the Authors

Sung Min Park (sm28386@skku.edu) is currently an associate professor in the Department of Public Administration & Graduate School of Governance at Sungkyunkwan University (SKKU). He has also served as assistant professor in the Greenspun School of Environmental and Public Affairs (SEPA) at the University of Nevada in Las Vegas. Park conducts research on management and human resource management in the public sector, focusing on leadership; values and motivations; organizational culture and structure; organizational behavior and performance; human resource development; IT management; and human resource information systems in the public, private, and nonprofit sectors. His academic work appears in American Review of Public Administration; Review of Public Personnel Administration; International Public Management Journal; Public Personnel Management; International Review of Administrative Sciences; Public Management Review; International Journal of Human Resource Management; and International Review of Public Administration. In 2005, Sung Min Park received Sage Publications' Best Doctoral Conference Paper Award presented by the Public and Nonprofit Division of the Academy of Management. In 2006, Bill Collins Award for the outstanding doctoral student paper was presented to him at the 2006 Southeastern Conference for Public Administration. In 2008, he received the 2007 Review of Public Personnel Administration (ROPPA) Best Article Award, conferred jointly by the American Society for Public Administration and Sage Publications. In the same year, he also received the 2007 Academy of Management (AOM) PNP Division Best Dissertation Award. In 2013, when he returned to Korea, he received the SKKU-Fellowship (Young Fellow) Award for Excellence in Research and Teaching, conferred by Sungkyunkwan University. Until now, Park has served as a director of the Global MPA Program in the Graduate School of Governance at SKKU and has worked as a managing editor of Korean Social Science Journal. He is also serving as a guest reviewer/referee of a wide range of internationally renowned ISI indexed journals. He received his B.A. degree from Yonsei University in 1997 (from the Department of Political Science and International Studies) and his M.I.A. degree from Columbia University in 2002 (from the School of International and Public Affairs).

He continued his formal education until 2007 when he received his Ph.D. degree from the University of Georgia (from the Department of Public Administration and Policy in the School of Public and International Affairs).

Seona Kim (seona1203@skku.edu) is a Ph.D. candidate in the Graduate School of Governance at Sungkyunkwan University. She also serves as an adjunct professor at Anyang University. She has lectured on "Human Relations Approach", "Understanding Social Science", "Understanding Korean Economy" and etc. Her primary research topics include public management, public human resource management, and organizational behavior. As a token of her outstanding academic achievements, she has published numerous articles such as "Determinants of Job Satisfaction and Turnover Intentions of Public Employees: Evidence from US Federal Agencies" (International Review of Public Administration, 2014), "Unveiling the Relationship among Job Choice Motivation, Job Satisfaction and Turnover Intention in the Public and Private Sector: With a focus on a Moderating Role of Person-Job Fit" (A Study on Korean Public Administration, 2013), "An Empirical Study on Organizational Performance in the Public Sector: With a focus on Managerial Roles of Social Capital and Knowledge Management Activities" (Journal of Policy Analysis And Evaluation, 2013), and "An Analysis of the Impacts of WLB Policies and Policy Congruence on Organizational Effectiveness: With a focus on Comparing Public and Private sector Organizations" (Korean Public Administration Review, 2013).

Preface

This case handbook will give important insights and practical tools in understanding organizational trends, realities, and tenets distinct in the public sector. Today's public organizations are adopting various organizational management mechanisms dramatically different from those a decade ago—that is, it require much more creative actions, intelligent judgment, and effective decision-making.Based on broad theoretical and practical issues, this book was designed to impart profound and comprehensive lessons on public organizational management. This book adopted Dr. Hal G. Rainey's "A Framework for Organizational Analysis" (2009, p. 19-23) and framed the topics into 8 sections and 8 key themes, which includes (1) Auspices: Public, Nonpublic, and so on; (2) Environments; (3) Leadership; (4) Culture; (5) Structures; (6) Processes; (7) People; and (8) Organizational Performance and Effectiveness. The book emphasizes on the implication of various issues at the "micro" (i.e., internal issues) and "macro" (i.e., external issues concerning relations and strategy) levels in an organization. This book also discusses important aspects of effective management in public organizations.

Specifically, the book introduces various types of cases and discussion questions pertaining to the issues of public organization and management, such as virtual/role play & simulation cases, problem-based learning (PBL) cases, and actual agency analysis cases. The case studies prompt discussion on a number of topics, including but not limited to the administrative environments, authority and structures, managing for effectiveness, leadership and culture, and the relationship between government and nonprofit organizations. The discussion/PBL questions and class exercises that follow the case studies are linked to the topics illustrated in each section. These case studies and questions can be used in the class to prompt discussions on key themes or assigned to students as homework. At the end of each section, relevant research notes/ frameworks are provided in order to give readers access to the key research issues. In the Appendix, a different set of public agency websites have been included to guide and facilitate class activities, for example, developing group application project papers and presentations. This book is expected to serve as a useful reference source for academics and researchers, a guide for public managers, policy makers, and practitioners, and as a teaching resource for undergraduate and graduate courses.

| C o n t e n t s |

Auspices

Framework

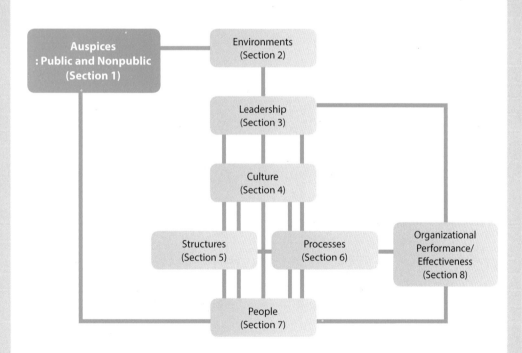

Source: Park, S. M. (2013). *Public Management: A Research Handbook*. Daeyoung Moonhwasa Publishing Company.

Keyword

- Public
- Management
- Public Organization
- Private Organization
- Public Management
- Public Values
- Public Interest
- Public Goods
- Organizational Theory
- Organizational Behavior

- Market Failure
- Free Riders
- Individual Incompetence
- Externalities
- Spillovers

1 Role Play Simulation

1. Play One's Role as a Public Administrator

Connecticut Department of Transportation

At a Glance

JAMES F. BYRNES, JR., Commissioner
James A. Adams, Deputy Commissioner
Established – 1969
Statutory authority – CGS P.A. 69-768
Authorized number of full-time employees – 3,751
Recurring operating expenses - $363.5 million
Capital budget - $723.7 million

Organizational Structure

Office of the Commissioner, Bureau of Aviation and Ports, Bureau of Finance and Administration, Bureau of Engineering and Highway Operations, Bureau of Policy and Planning, Bureau of Public Transportation, State Traffic Commission.

Mission

To provide a safe, efficient and cost-effective transportation system that meets the mobility needs of its users.

Statutory Responsibility

The agency shall be responsible for all aspects of the planning, development, maintenance and improvement of transportation in the state (Section 13b-3 C.G.S.).

The agency serves its customers by providing safe and efficient systems for the movement of people and goods within, to or from the state, whether by highway, air, water, rail or other means (Section 13b-2I).

Information Reported as Required by State Statute

The agency shall develop and revise, biennially, a comprehensive long-range transportation plan designed to fulfill the present and future needs of the state and to assure the development and maintenance of an adequate, safe and efficient transportation system (Section 13b-15 C.G.S). The purpose of the Master Transportation Plan is to provide its customers, the Administration, the General Assembly, local elected officials, and the general public with a comprehensive understanding of the transportation projects and programs that the agency will be pursuing over the next ten years. The strategic goals of the agency are to ensure safety, maintain the existing system, increase system productivity, promote economic development and provide required capacity.

Affirmative Action Policy

It is the established policy of the Department to guarantee equal employment opportunity and to implement affirmative action programs.

Improvements/Achievements 2002-03

Bradley International Airport's terminal improvement program focused on completion of the new Unified Terminal.

The Bureau of Aviation and Ports worked with Bradley's Board of Directors to implement new marketing programs including a redesigned website and refined media ads.

Through a public/private partnership, a new control tower was opened at Waterbury-Oxford Airport staffed by the FAA.

The Department continued to manage all programs and projects to maximize federal funds allocated to Connecticut for improvements to all transportation facilities. Significant completed projects include: reconstruction of I-95 in Stamford; and construction of a 50,000-square-foot warehouse designed for heavy cargo at the Admiral Harold E. Shear State Pier in New London.

The Bureau of Engineering and Highway Operations continued to manage all programs and projects to maximize federal funds allocated to Connecticut for improvements to all transportation facilities. Significant completed projects include: replacement of the Tomlinson Bridge in New Haven; reconstruction of I-95 interchange 56 in Branford; resurfacing of I-91 in Windsor Locks and resurfacing of I-84 in West Hartford.

The largest capital program within the Department's current plan is the I-95 New Haven Harbor Crossing Corridor Improvement Program. The program includes both roadway and transit improvements to increase capacity and reduce congestion between New Haven and Branford.

A new commuter railroad station at State Street in New Haven was opened last year and the Branford portion of the highway reconstruction is well under way. Additional contracts will proceed to construction in East Haven and New Haven in the coming year. The entire program will occur in stages through 2012.

The Department is also developing a preliminary design for a new transit system, the New Britain-Hartford Busway. Upon completion of the preliminary design and securing the necessary funding, a design-build contract will be advertised and awarded to complete the final design and construct the busway.

The Bureau of Policy and Planning completed major planning studies for I-84 (from the New York state line to Waterbury and Hartford); Truck Stop and Rest Area Parking; Feeder Barge Feasibility; and Intrastate Passenger Ferry Service

Feasibility. The Bureau also initiated studies for Statewide Airport Systems; I-95 Southeast Corridor; and the New Haven to Springfield Commuter Rail Service Feasibility.

The Bureau of Policy and Planning provided extensive support for the Transportation Strategy Board (TSB) program initiatives, studies and projects.

The Bureau of Public Transportation developed an Implementation Plan for a Bus Rapid Transit (BRT) System for the capital area from New Britain to Hartford.

The Bureau of Policy and Planning conducts planning activities for transit, highways, goods movement, commuter parking, bicycle and recreation, airports, and performs environmental analysis for all projects. The Bureau also coordinates statewide transportation planning activities with the Regional Planning Agencies.

The Bureau of Policy and Planning administered programs for commuter parking facilities and pedestrian and bicyclist needs. Continuing major studies include Statewide Airport Systems Plan; I-95 Branford – Rhode Island; New Haven-Springfield Commuter Rail Service; Rail Station and Parking Governance; I-95 Commuter Shoulder and Hartford East Bus Rapid Transit. Major studies initiated include Danbury Branch Electrification; I-84/Route 8 Interchange; Oxford Airport Master Plan.

The Bureau of Policy and Planning published the 2003 Master Transportation Plan and provided extensive support for the Transportation Strategy Board (TSB) program initiatives, studies and projects.

The Bureau of Public Transportation's mission is to provide mobility to the residents of the state and to enhance economic development, access to jobs and the environment by providing safe, efficient, economical, and reliable transportation alternatives. Significant improvements/achievements include:

· Development and maintenance of a fiscally constrained Transit Capital Plan that fully programs all state and federal funds expected to be made available over a 20-year horizon.
· Development of condition studies and structural improvement plans for the state's railroad bridges.
· Rehabilitation of a significant portion of the state's rail rolling stock to maintain reliable service schedules.
· Continuation of major study to determine the next generation of rail rolling stock needed.
· Completion of the New Haven Interlocking project, a major reconfiguration of the tracks serving New Haven Terminal to allow for improved commuter operations and for Northeast Corridor express trains.
· Purchase of replacement buses for the Connecticut Transit System and Southeast Area Transit.
· Investigation of opportunities for innovative financing programs such as design/build.

Source: The case was written by Dr. Hal G. Rainey

Warm-Up Questions

1   Define the scope of the organization.

2   The DOT organizational structure includes several other entities, namely: Office of the Commissioner, Bureau of Aviation and Ports, Bureau of Finance and Administration, Bureau of Engineering and Highway Operations, Bureau of Policy and Planning, Bureau of Public Transportation, and the State Traffic Commission. Information on the purpose and function of these other agencies is included in the text. Are the lines of authority and relationships clear? If possible, draw an organization chart showing the relationships. Would you describe the DOT as a closed or open organization? Explain.

3   Who heads the agency?

4   What are the main functions of the DOT?

5   What are the main functions of the associated agencies (see organizational structure)?

6   What private entities might rely on the agency?

7   Is the mission statement clear or ambiguous? Explain.

8   Consider the mission of each associated entity. In your opinion, do any missions conflict? Can you determine the importance of the agencies from the structure itself?

9   What projects in the state are most important?

10 Who are the agency's main stakeholders?

11 The mission statement reads,–The agency shall be responsible for–all aspects of the planning, development, maintenance and improvement of transportation in the state. How do you think the agency determines the relative importance of different modes of transportation? For example, is bus transportation more important than rail transportation?

12 From the text, list the main tasks of leaders within the main organization.

13 Is there a strong–chain of command?

14 In what ways is–flexibility built into the organization? Do priorities change year to year?

15 Would–one best way work in this organization?

16 Do the different subunits face the same environment or different environments?

17 What oversight mechanisms can you find within the information on the agency?

18 What principles of–sound management can you identify within the information.

19 What, if anything, can you determine about the culture of the agency?

20 What, if anything, can you determine about the values of the organization?

Source: The discussion questions were based on the case written by Dr. Hal G. Rainey

2. Play One's Role as a Government Reformer

Let's suppose you are appointed as the manager of Task Force Reform (TFR), a special unit under the Ministry of Public Management of Korea. The main objective for the formulation of the task force is to lead the government reorganization plan. Below is a memorandum via email addressed to your task force directing your group to draft the government's comprehensive reform plan and submit the same to the Minister. Please read the memorandum and let's try to address the issues asked.

> **From** Minister Sup-Jong Cho (minsiter_mpm@korea.com) You moved this message to its current location.
>
> **Sent** Thursday, July 24, 2014 3:34:29 PM
>
> **To** Task Force Reform (taskforcereform_mpm@korea.com)
>
> 2 attachment | Download all as zip (1234.0 KB) Comprehensive Government Reform Plan.docx (698.0 KB) Dealing with Korea's Bureaucracy.docx (536.0 KB)
>
> View online
>
> MEMORANDUM-MPM0001
>
> TO: Task Force Reform (TFR)
> RE: Submission of Comprehensive Government Reform Plan
> FROM: The Minister, Ministry of Public Management
> DATE: 24 July 2014
>
> -
>
> The growing public condemnation on the government's shortcomings is going beyond our borders now. World's views on our pressing public organization and bureaucratic issues are reverberating across the nation. As a government official,

we can't just take all these things pass through our senses.

The public clamor commands us to implement government reforms. Yes, indeed, there is a need to initiate important changes in our public management and the entire bureaucracy.

Thus, I hereby direct your unit, Task Force Reform, to draft and submit a "Comprehensive Government Reform Plan" that must include general and specific reform agenda for the whole government system. I would like you to give a serious attention and provide an elaborate response on the following issues:

a. How would you define public and public interest?
b. Comparing with other countries, what are the unique characteristics of public and nonprofit agencies in Korea?
c. What are the main philosophical and cultural underpinnings of Korean public management?
d. In terms of organizational effectiveness and performance, what are the positive and negative aspects of such managerial characteristics?
e. The possible problems that may arise from such characteristics, and then share ideas on how to resolve and overcome these issues.

For your immediate action and compliance.

Attached File 1: Problem-Based Learning (PBL)

Comprehensive Government Reform Plan

	Step	Contents		
1	Environments/ Conditions/ Backgrounds	Please explain the situation briefly.		
2	Problem Definition	In your own perspective, please be as specific as possible when pointing out the problem.		
3	Actual Case Studies	Please explain by giving specific examples (Newspaper articles, news clips, or interviews)		
4	Finding Alternatives	Possible Solutions	Merits/Pros in a Korean Context	Demerits/Cons in a Korean Context
		①		
		②		
		③		
5	The Best Solution	Why did you choose this alternative as the best solution? What are the expected effects and potential contribution?		

 **Attached File 2**

Dealing with Korea's Bureaucracy

...Bureaucrats anywhere are infamous for maintaining the status quo. But change can and does happen. Contrary to many foreigners' expectations, the real power for change normally does not take place at the minister lever. Rather, it is most commonly found in the bureaucracy at the director (samugwan) and deputy subdirector (gwajang) levels. Although those holding these positions are relatively low in the bureaucratic hierarchy, they are the gatekeepers. Only by their direct involvement do all documents move upwards to the ministers who make the actual decisions. They are personally responsible for specific bodies of regulations. At the same time, like their counterparts in other countries, the bureaucrat's primary instinct is for self-preservation. Under the bureaucratic system, as long as one does not make major blunders, one's position is usually secure.

The three things that mid-level bureaucrats do not wish are 1) to be discovered by internal and external government auditors making the wrong decisions; 2) to hear from their senior officials that the director generals are saying "you are making my life miserable;" and 3) to cause their ministry to be chastised by the press — or be questioned by higher-level government bodies, including the presidential or prime ministerial offices. Officials, therefore, naturally tend to be quite prudent in handling affairs in the private business sector, lest a hasty decision cause some adverse repercussions and thus jeopardize their position. ...

... Given the above, the best thing a bureaucrat can do is to do nothing or be convinced that something needs to be done as a defense against the above-stated pressures. Consequently, whatever strategy one employs to change a regulation, it is normally essential to take the time and effort for long-term education of the middle bureaucracy. Though one may often get the impression that officials are "dragging their feet" — or are being evasive or non-committal, one must keep in mind that officials are overly sensitive about the long-term security of their positions. ...

Source: The information contained in this article was extracted from
"The Korea Times (2008.01.24)" by Coyner, T.

2 Theory Synopsis

1. Conceptualizing Public Organizations

One of the most daunting issues in distinguishing public from a private organization is the absence of a clear definition of public organization. We may ask, what really constitute public organization? Do public organizations solely denote government agencies? How about organizations that provides public service for the sake of public interest? Can we classify them as public organization?

Some researchers and theorists denote public organization as government agencies clothed with legal status in which the citizens have a major stake (see, for example, Rainey, 1979). There are those who argue that, emphasizing not on the legal status of a certain organization, but rather on the "matter of the economic character of the goods or services delivered" will determine whether or not an organization falls under the category of a public organization (Bozeman, 1987, p. 4). The distinction between public and private organizations can advance by identifying the core sets of government organizations—core government; and the core sets that are identified from the private sector, the so-called core business (Rainey, Backoff, & Levine, 1976). In this approach, the basic criterion is the legal status of the organization that is usually classified as public and private. The comparison through the core approach clarifies that there are significant differences in the administration and conduct of public and private organizations.

Without a clear and unambiguous conceptualization of public organization, we may think that all organizations can either be public or private. Different conceptions of public organizations from various experts, researchers, and theorists holding valid and logical assertions cause confusion and inconclusive use of the concept. The vagueness not only result to the haphazard conceptualization of public organization, but also marooned the distinction between public and private in uncertain terms. But is it really possible to draw a demarcation line between public and private organizations? Rainey

(2009) doesn't agree with such idea. He claimed that, "oversimplified distinctions between public and private organizations are misleading" (Rainey, 2009, p. 66).

2. The Raison d'etre for Public Organizations

1) Political Hierarchies and Economic Market

Public organizations evolve to meet societal need, and apparently, to provide public service for the public good. There are many practical reasons, however, we can draw a profound explanation of the existence of public organizations drawing from the political and economic theories. Robert Dahl and Charles Lindblom (1953) provided an effective tool for the analysis of the existence of public organizations using economic/market and political authority.

In the analysis of Dahl and Lindblom (1953), they identified two critical alternatives that best explain the existence of public organizations: political hierarchies (also known as polyarchy) and economic markets.

First, drawing from the political authority, the political hierarchies or polyarchy is an effective means of social control that direct an individual or entity to act in accordance with a settled law, ordinance, or regulations. An individual or an entity complies or act under certain conditions, if any, to the impositions laid by political hierarchies. Thus, it seems not easy to understand the political authority because compliance might be due to some factors like fear of coercive power granted to lawful authorities, recognition and respect of the state and its existing laws, complaisance that is an inherent commitment to traditions, political community, and political habits, or a reciprocal response to quality of service (Rothschild, 1977; Friedrich, 1963; Cochran, 1977; Merelman, 1977; as cited in Bozeman, 1987).

Second, Dahl and Lindblom (1953) argue that markets have the advantage of existing through a voluntary or willful exchange process between producers and consumers. In the production of consumer's need, public organizations have the incentive to identify and efficiently work for the consumers. This encourages autonomy, creativity, innovation, and flexibility as against the hierarchical and rule making that are essential in a polyarchy.

The interaction of political hierarchies and economic activities is prevalent in all countries. In advanced industrial democracies, the political process is characterized by a strong and convoluted interplay of various interest groups and institutions that generates a complex, multi-faceted, and branched hierarchies.

2) Public Values and Public Interest

The public value approach, that has been articulated by various researchers and theorists, is gaining considerable interest as a new method for meeting the challenges of efficiency, accountability, democracy, and as a rationale for the existence of public organizations. But, what is public value? For Bozeman (2007), he defined public value as, "a society's 'public values' are those providing normative consensus about (1) the rights, benefits, and prerogatives to which citizens should (and should not) be entitled; (2) the obligations of citizens to society, the state, and one another; and (3) the principles in which governments and policies should be based (p. 13). Public value can be understood as the value or importance citizens attach to the outcome of government policies and their experience of public services (Moore, 1994).

Public sector organizations produce value when they meet the needs of citizens—the higher the level of needs satisfied, the higher the amount of public value created (Moore, 1995). The creation of public value reflects what people think about and feel towards the society to which they belong. In this broad sense, the definition of public value interfaces with the need to develop models and tools to encourage dialogue on shared values between the parties, to manage conflicting values, to define the role of the public sector in transforming social contexts (Meinhardt & Metelmann, 2009).

In the 1995 book of Mark Moore entitled "Creating Public Value", he positioned himself within the ambit of the new tradition of public entrepreneurship rather than traditional public management—which, for him, is 'downward' rather than 'outward' oriented (Moore, 1995, p. 17). Moore identifies what's acknowledged to be a problem endemic to public management: objectives and performance indices are hard to specify. He writes 'in the public sector the overall aim of managerial work seems less clear; what managers need to do is produce value far more ambiguous; and how to measure whether value has been created far more difficult' (Moore, 1995, p. 28). However, unlike NPM, which 'solved' this problem by bringing public sector organizations closer to the operational practices of the private sector, Moore insists on the irreducible difference between public and private sectors: 'the aim of managerial work in the public sector is to create public value just as the aim of managerial work in the private sector is to create private National Consumer Council value' (Moore, 1995, p. 28).

For Moore (1995) public managers create public value. Managers can either deploy both resources and authority in order to create value for particular beneficiaries, or can establish and operate an institution that will give venue that meets citizens and their representatives for an effective and productive institution (p. 52). However, the problem is that they cannot know for sure what public value can be derived. Even if they could be sure today, they would have to doubt tomorrow, for by then the political aspirations and public needs that give points to their efforts might well have changed (Moore, 1995, p. 57).

Here lies the importance of Moore's case studies: they show public value to be more than, and different from, the realization of easily quantifiable outputs, for example, the number of houses built or the number of convictions achieved. Moore's accounts of the Boston Housing Authority's delivery of public value by transforming 'desperate individuals' to a "functioning competent community" and the Houston Police Department's 'production of community order' flesh out the concept (Moore, 1995, p. 222). He emphasizes the 'co-production' of outcomes achieved by public managers and public authorities working together with their clients. Indeed the essence of co-production, and successful creation of public value, is dissolution of the boundaries between client and provider which thereby augments the legitimacy of the organizations in question by strengthening their accountability to those whom they serve.

Moore's conception of public value, thus assigns an active role to users, whereby they behave as 'citizens acting through politics, rather than consumers acting through markets (Moore, 1995, p. 44)' and as citizens they 'establish both the level and distribution of production' (Moore, 1995, p. 44). Moore's insistence on the centrality of the user involves a distinction (Moore, 1995, p. 48) between the user as a consumer, who seeks what's good for her/himself and the user as citizen who seeks what's good for society. Moore acknowledges that this re-conceptualization of the user necessitates a complementary rethinking of public managers' role because 'the classic tradition of public administration does not focus a managers' attention on questions of purpose and value or on the development of legitimacy and support (Moore, 1995, p. 74).

Kelly et al. (2002) define three key building blocks of public value: services, outcomes, and trust. Public services are critical in the creation of value as they represent the vehicle for the delivery of fairness, equity and other values in actual service encounters with the citizen. These building blocks provide for a new way of thinking about the evaluation of government activity, as a new conceptualization of the public interest is defined in an effort to better balance efficiency and effectiveness (O'Flynn, 2007; Stoker, 2006).

3) Market Failures

The rationale for the existence of public organizations is to create and produce public values—meeting the needs of citizens and ensuring protection from the perils of various political and economic market limitations. The concept of public value creation and the stabilization of economic interplay between the capital and market are similar. However, authors determining the failures in the economic market exchange were given less attention by which public values are compromised to a greater extent. Some of the issues, if not taken into serious account, may engender economic market failure are the following: 1) public goods and free riders, 2) individual incompetence, and 3) externalities or spillovers (Rainey, 2009).

First, in the creation and delivery of public goods, the primordial goal is to bring benefit to all. In the process, free riders—those who acts in private capacity benefits from the resources, public goods, and services without cost, but let others pay for it—are allowed to pitch in. For example, private entities may engage in providing training and security services, which is a 'must be' delivered public good by the government. Interested parties or clienteles may engage the services of a private service provider but will pay for the service cost. The government levies appropriate taxes for the free riders (service provider) and provide regulatory measures similar to other business activities.

Second, citizens may lack sufficient knowledge, skill, or information in making a wise decision in some areas of its economic market interaction. For example, people can't possibly determine appropriate medications to a particular illness, thus the government through the Professional Regulatory Commission or board regulates and screens medical practitioners that will skillfully and professionally deal with any body ailment or disability.

Third, there are cost or benefits that may spill over upon the citizens who did not opt to incur such cost or benefit. It may not be a serious issue, or no issue at all, if a market exchange muster positive externality instead of cost or negative spillover. For example, air pollution caused by manufacturing companies, imposes costs on others that the price of the product does not cover. Thus, the government through its Environmental Protection Agency, Department of Health, or authorized government entity must regulate the operations and impose proper measures to such externalities.

3. What is Public?

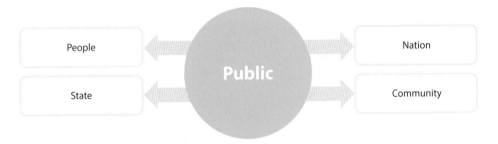

The term public originates from the Latin word "populus" or "poplicus" which generally denotes people, nation, state, community. Out from such conceptualization, public can be collectively denoted as the people who constitute a nation, state, or community. The concept of public is defined differently and used in different ways in various contexts. For example, in the field of political science, public is denoted as a mass population within a civic or community affairs; and can also be denoted as the affairs of the state. In the public relations and social psychology, public is denoted as a self-creating and self-organizing group of people, having a common or shared interest and that they grouped themselves to address issues relating it. Some authors describe public as either situational—people are organized because of a triggering situation (Dewey, 1927) or non-situational—active or passive interaction of a group with an organization or between people in the group (Hallahah, 2000). One of the most common and popular usage of the term public equates with governmental affairs (Bozeman, 1987) just like public organizations being equated with governmental bureaus (Peabody & Rourke, 1965; as cited in Perry & Rainey, 1988).

The term private is derived from the Latin word "privatus" which means unofficial, a private person, or that is to be deprived of public office or separation from government on some personal considerations. Private organizations are oftentimes "identified as all other organizations, or as business firms bureaus (Peabody & Rourke, 1965; as cited in Perry & Rainey, 1988) The conceptualization of the word private may be understood by drawing a demarcation line that defines the capacity to represent a legal authority. Being private, the juridical capacity of a person, entity, or an institution may stem from a statutory accreditation or legal recognition to perform lawful acts for private or limited interest and sometimes for a consideration. Being public, on the other hand, the juridical capacity of a person, entity, or an institution emanates from the governmental power granted by a law or statute for public interest. It can also be understood that public acts are considered government acts, while private acts are deemed as acts in a personal capacity.

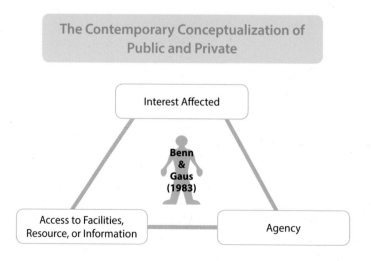

Moreover, in the contemporary conceptualization of public and private, three major factors are considered (Benn & Gaus, 1983): (1) interest affected—whether it is shared or restricted to individuals; (2) access to facilities, resources, or information; and (3) agency—whether the act done is personal in nature or for the public interest. These characteristic dimensions may be a stand-alone, a collective factor, or may even be a contrasting factor. For example, the national security plan of Korea, which is prepared by the Ministry of National Defense to ensure safety and security of the general public against foreign intrusion. The ministry acting as the agent of the state may deny access to such information to avoid possible leakage to enemy state(s) and compromise the general security plan.

4. What is Management?

What is the meaning of management? Is it the same, in a broader or narrower sense than administration? Can we distinguish management with administration, leadership, entrepreneurship, and implementation? Are these concepts the same? In the public organization context, who are considered public managers? What about in the private organization, who are the private managers? Basically, these questions will give light to the core elements and characteristics of management, drawing from the perspective of public and private organizations.

Dictionaries defined management as pertaining to the act or manner of managing—handling, directing, controlling, or supervising resources to achieve a desired result. In the article "Notes on the Theory of Organization," Gulick (1937) presented two fundamental functions of management: (1) division of labor and (2) work coordination. Concerning the division of labor, he emphasized on the need of a well-defined specialization of labor. According to him, by specialization, it allows the matching of skills and tasks; and the clear delineation of tasks. However, Gulick noted three limitations on specialization. First, no job should be so specialized that would not take a full time of a worker, in which case the worker need to have had other work to fill their working time. Second, certain technological conditions, traditions or customs may constrain the assignment of tasks. Third, intricately related tasks must not be separated from each other.

Under the work coordination, Gulick proposed methods to achieve coordination of divided labor. Work can be coordinated either through organization—placing workers under the supervision of a manager or through dominance of an idea—a clear direction of what is to be done in each work, and that workers fit the task and unites efforts. For coordination through organization, Gulick pointed some important principles that must be considered. One of the principles is that, the span of control or subordinates reporting to one supervisor must be narrow or controlled. Some authors have settled on the ratio of subordinates and supervisors between six and ten. However, he noted that the number of subordinates in every supervisor depends on some organizational factors such as stability, subordinates specialization which matched with the supervisor. Gulick also proposed the principle of "one master"—each subordinate should serve only one master. There must be unity of command so as to avoid confusion and work inefficiency. Another principle is the homogeneity principle—dissimilar tasks must not be grouped together. Gulick pointed out that identical tasks must clustered accordingly and that a specialized group must be supervised by homogenous specialist.

In the same classic paper, Gulick summarized the job of management and administration through what became one of the most popular and influential acronym in management: POSDCORB. The letters stand for: (1) planning; (2) organizing; (3) staffing; (4) directing; (5) coordinating; (6) reporting; and (7) budgeting.

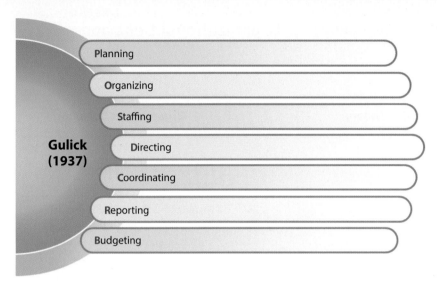

Gulick (1937)
- Planning
- Organizing
- Staffing
- Directing
- Coordinating
- Reporting
- Budgeting

Ever since the early management and contemporary theorists tries to describe the role of the managers or administrators using the guiding principles of planning, organizing, staffing, directing, coordinating, reporting, and budgeting (POSDCORB) or some variant of it to define what managers must do. There is a repeated notion that, managers in all settings must do pretty much the same types of work. Allison (1983) illustrated the managerial responsibilities, drawing from the guiding conception of POSDCORB.

In the classic study of the U.S. Office of Personnel Management (OPM), they developed questions that sought to identify the important skills for public managers. The questions were categorized into two competency dimensions: (1) management functions and (2) effectiveness.

Functions The "What" of Management	Effectiveness The "How" of Management
- External Awareness	- Broad Perspective
- Interpretation	- Strategic View
- Representation	- Environmental Sensitivity
- Coordination	- Leadership
- Work Unit Planning	- Flexibility
- Work Unit Guidance	- Action Orientation
- Budgeting	- Results Focus
- Material Resources Administration	- Communication
- Personnel Management	- Interpersonal Sensitivity
- Supervision	- Technical Competence
- Work Unit Monitoring	
- Program Evaluation	

Source: Flanders & Utterback (1985, p. 405)

5. Organizational Theory vs. Organizational Behavior

Organization Theory		Organization Behavior
• Based in sociology		• Primary origins in industrial and social psychology
• Focus in on topics that concern the organization as a whole, such as environments, goals and effectiveness, structure and design, strategy, etc.		• Focus is on individual and group behavior – motivation, work dynamic, attitudes and behavior, etc.
		• Integrates interventions and similar practice techniques

1) Organizational Theory

Organizational theory focuses on the study of organizational structures, the organization and its relationship with the external environment, and the relationship of factors within the organization such as leadership behavior, organizational behavior, and among other studies and fields. Organizational theory provides organizational coping mechanism from different challenges in work and organization.

In a broader sense, the study of organizational theory provides an encompassing normative theories that helps identify issues that affects organizational performance by identifying organizational patterns and structures. Some argue that in order to run an organization, public or private organization, one must clearly understand the dynamics of organizational theory and apply it in real world organization management.

2) Organizational Behavior

Organizational behavior is defined as "the study of individuals and groups within an organizational context, and the study of internal processes and practices as they influence the effectiveness of individuals, teams, and organizations" (Slocum & Hellriegel, 2011, p. 4). Organizational behavior deals with the understanding of human behavior—interaction of individuals, groups, organization, and broader system— to improve the performance of organizations and the people in them. Some authors described the organizational behavior as a study that focuses on "human behavior and individual values rather than organizational structures and organizational values" and "is not just a field of study; it is a way of thinking and acting that is of critical importance and value to people who work in public organizations" (Denhardt, Denhardt, & Artisgueta, 2013, p. 2 & 6). Denhardt et al. (2013) further emphasized that organizational behavior deals practically with all aspects of organizations and management in the standpoint of the individual.

In the public sector, organizational behavior can be described as the study of how people in the public organizations behave or act, work motivation, and their interaction with each other. It can be seen through the interaction of the individual behavior, group behavior, organizational factors, and the public sector environment.

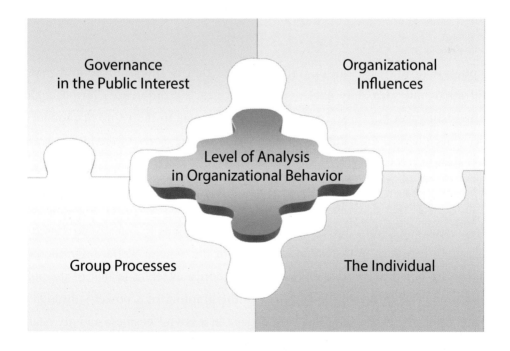

Source: Denhardt et al. (2013, p. 6)

In the stages of organizational behavior analysis, the individual factor served as the foundation of the whole process analysis. Organizational behavior posits that in order to improve performance of people in the organization, understanding individual behavior is critical because it is the inner behavioral interactions that determines people's behavior in a group, in an organization, and in the whole social system. The emphasis of organizational behavior on individual human behavior and values rather than organizational structures and values makes it distinct field while having a common perspective with organizational theory.

6. Threats to Private and Public Management

The pursuit in drawing the demarcation line that defines public and private organizations line seemingly does not give any clear-cut difference. Various authors tried to distinguish public and private organizations as to the value of products or services they provide, the nature of such services, and the extent of the impact it gives to the citizens.

In some respect, the distinctions were oftentimes defined as to the legal authority that represents the will of the citizens. Public organizations manifestly possessed the legal baton to identify projects and activities for the general welfare. On the other hand, private organizations are clothed with authority different to that of the public organization. The nature of the authority is the granting of a power—through the regulatory police power of the state—to engage in a lawful business activity gearing towards profit.

Others also emphasize not on the legal status of the organization, rather on the matter economic character of the goods or services delivered. The core of the public organization is government service to the people, while in the private organization, the core is on the business that demands an exchange of economic goods through a consideration. Succeeding discussions in this section will detail the difference of public and private based on previous studies and the underlying threats that challenges their existence.

7. Characteristics of Public Organization

In the face of continuous debate on different streams of arguments in public and private organization, an increasing part of the private and public organizations literature is an evidence providing a clear demarcation of both sectors. There has been a remarkable leap in the research, however the basic contentions that draw the distinction controversy still remains. Based on the articles "Comparing Public and Private Organizations," Rainey, Backoff, and Levine (1976) presented a summary of common assertions and research findings on the differences between public and private organizations. They emphasized that the point of consensus is organized into various categories: environmental factors, propositions about transactions of organizations with their environment, then to propositions concerning factors within organizations, including the individual in the organization.

1) Environmental Factors

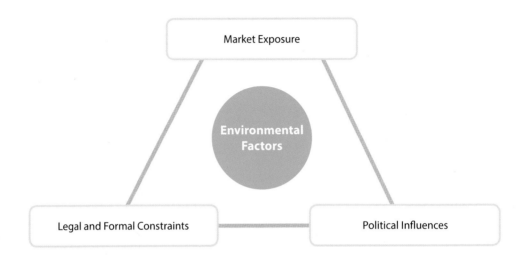

Various factors that are external to organizations are described as environmental factors. The arguments from various authors identified these factors—market exposure, legal and formal constraints, and political influence—as critical in the identification of distinctive characteristics of public management.

Market Exposure. The difference between public and private organizations stems from their involvement or non-involvement with the economic market as a source of "resources, information, and constraints." Public organizations obtain the resources via budget allocation in an appropriation process within a political context. The dynamics of a political process and government behavioral approach of governance warrants the adoption of market-type concepts of management to stir public organization's efficiency.

Legal and Formal Constraints. Various authors cite public and private differences on the impact of formal and rigid legal system in public organizations especially in relations to autonomy and flexibility. In the private organizations, the only thing that is required of them is the lawful compliance of laws, statutes, or ordinances with regard the conduct of their business or activities. However, transactions, management, decision-making, and other governmental activities are governed by implementing procedures as provided by laws, statutes, administrative orders (AOs), executive orders (EOs), judicial orders or court rulings in the public organizations. Others denote this as "legalism" and "legal habit." These characteristics are governed by the traditional and bureaucratic management approach.

Political Influences. Public organizations are not insulated from political influences when it comes to decision and/or policy-making, for example "political bargaining and lobbying, public opinion, interest-group, client, and constituent pressures." There is a need for political support of the client groups, citizens, and formal authorities to obtain resources and authorization.

2) Organization-Environment Transactions

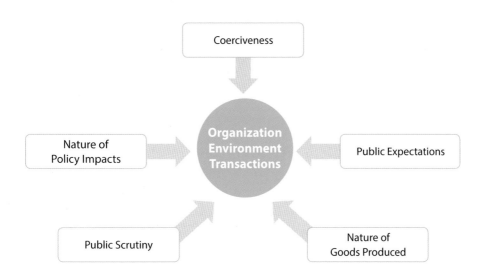

Some of the distinguishing points between private and public organizations is their relationship to different entities surrounding them.

Coerciveness. The basic distinction between public and private organization is the coercive power that is available solely for the former. Public organizations can levy taxes from the citizens to finance governmental activities, that is constitutionally justifiable and an extensive formal control mechanism.

Nature of Policy Impacts. To compare the public and private organization as to the breadth of scope, impact, and consideration. Various authors contend that public organizations have a greater extent of impact than private organizations.

Public Scrutiny. Public organizations can't escape from public scrutiny. Private organizations may not be insulated to such public scrutiny, but the degree is not that encompassing like with public organizations. The difference can be traced from the perception that public organizations are being owned by the "state and citizens, thus citizens have the right to scrutinize it which they don't have it with private organizations.

Public Expectations. In relation to public scrutiny, the perceived ownership of citizens to public organizations gives them the right to expect more from the government in terms of "integrity, fairness, responsiveness, and accountability."

Nature of Goods Produced. Economists noted that, public organizations are involved in the production of "public goods"—excludes application of prices and market mechanism; and quasi-public goods—provided at a cost.

3) Organizational Roles, Structures, and Processes

Organizational Roles, Structures, and Processes

- Greater goal ambiguity, multiplicity, and conflict
- Distinctive features of general managerial roles
- Administrative authority and leadership practices
- Organizational structure
- Strategic decision-making processes
- Incentives and incentive structures
- Individual characteristics, work-related attitudes and behaviors
- Organization and individual performance

A number of assumptions emphasized on the roles, internal operations, and organizational structure, such as managerial roles, individual authority, and decision-making.

Greater goal ambiguity, multiplicity, and conflict. One of the distinct and commonly raised difference between public and private organization is the nature of "goals and performance measures." The differences are based on the following dimensions:

▶ Multiplicity and evaluation criteria
▶ Vagueness and intangibility
▶ Goal conflict

Distinctive features of general managerial roles. Studies revealed that public managerial roles include many of the same functions and role as those who are in the private organizations. However, public managers can be distinguished with the following leadership features:

▶ More political
▶ Expository role
▶ More meetings with and interventions of external interest groups and political authorities
▶ More crisis management and "fire drills"
▶ A greater challenge to a balance external and political relations with internal management functions.

Administrative authority and leadership practices. Recent studies indicate some prominent leadership practices and extent of administrative authority.

▶ Less decision-making autonomy and flexibility
▶ Weaker authority over subordinates
▶ Higher-level public managers show greater reluctance to delegate authority
▶ Frequent turnover due to elections and political appointments

► Entrepreneurial behaviors and managerial excellence.

Organizational structure. Various studies asserts that public organizations that it moved towards a more elaborate bureaucratic structure, thus subject to more red tape.

Strategic decision-making processes. Strategic decision-making processes in public organizations can be generally the same with the private organizations but are more exposed to interventions, interruptions, and involvement of other actors.

Incentives and incentive structures. Recent studies have provided that there is a difference in terms of administrative constraints with regards the extrinsic incentives (i.e., pay, promotion, and disciplinary action). Public managers and employees also perceived that there is a weaker relations between performance and extrinsic incentives.

Individual characteristics, work-related attitudes and behaviors. Research on the levels of work satisfaction and organizational commitment among public managers and employees found to be lower than among private managers and employees.

Organization and individual performance. There are numerous studies found that public managers and employees are "cautious and not innovative." There are also studies that public forms of various types of organizations tend to be less efficient than the other setting.

From Theory to Practice

1. Agency Analysis

Ministry of Security and Public Administration
vs.
SAMSUNG Group

Through the vision and strategy of public organization, it can readily be understood that its purpose is to promote public interest, public value, and publicness. Also, the comparison between public and private organization provide a greater understanding of the reason of existence of public organization. In this regard, we are going to look at the vision and strategy both of a public organization and a private organization. For the public organization, we will examine the case of the Ministry of Security and Public Administration (MOSPA); while in the private organization we will look at the case of the Samsung Group of companies.

The Ministry of Security and Public Administration (MOSPA) is one of the central government agencies of Korea. MOSPA assumes affairs related to national administration, government organization, personnel management, e-Government, and disaster safety. Furthermore, MOSPA actively supports the local government in terms of local administration, finance, and regional development for the promotion of greater local autonomy (www.mospa.go.kr/eng/a01/engMain.do).

Publicness of MOSPA is well emphasized in the vision. The MOSPA's overarching vision is the promotion of a safe society, a competent government, and the happiness of the people. Main strategy is categorized into eight types: 1) to establish a more capable government; 2) to foster trustworthy civil servants; 3) to ensure a safe and secure society; 4) to realize an advance knowledge-based information society; 5) to grant greater local autonomy to local governments; 6) to build an accountable fiscal management system for local governments; 7) to promote stabilization of people's lives by revitalizing local economy; and 8) to enhance government's organizational capacity. These strategies are essentially the same.

MOSPA must put utmost consideration on democracy, accountability and equity, and economic value; such as efficacy because public organization exists to enhance public interest and public values.

MOSPA's Vision and Strategy

The promotion of a safe society, a competent government, and the happiness of the people

to establish a more capable government	to foster trustworthy civil servants
to ensure a safe and secure society	to realize an advance knowledge-based information society
to grant greater local autonomy to local governments	to build an accountable fiscal management system for local governments
to promote stabilization of people's lives by revitalizing local economy	to enhance government's organizational capacity.

MOSPA

Samsung is one of the most powerful enterprises in the world. They engages in various businesses such as manufacturing, electronics, semiconductor, engineering, construction, distribution, insurance, pharmaceutical industry, among others.

Samsung Groups envisions developing innovative technologies and efficient processes that create new markets, enrich people's lives, and continue to make Samsung a digital leader. Along this vision, the company adopts five key values: 1) people; 2) excellence; 3) change; 4) integrity; and 5) co-prosperity.

SAMSUNG Group's Vision and Values

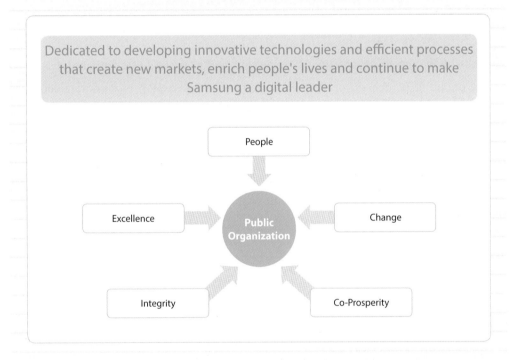

As a business or private enterprise, Samsung's goal is to earn profits through the best management and maximization of resources and company's five values. Valuing for "people", Samsung is dedicated on giving their people various opportunities to reach their full potentials. Giving importance for "excellence", Samsung is driven by an unyielding passion for excellence—and an unfaltering commitment to develop the best products and services available in the market.

As an important strategy for survival, Samsung Group values "change" or innovation to keep abreast on the demands and dominance of the market. Also, the company values "integrity" which emphasizes the importance of ethics in all its business operations. Finally, Samsung values "co-prosperity" or responsibility. Meaning, the company adheres to the principle that a business cannot be successful unless it creates prosperity and opportunity for others. Also, they are dedicated on bringing their company towards a socially and environmentally responsible corporate citizen in every community where they operate around the globe (www.samsung.com/us/).

The concept of co-prosperity in the private sector seems to be in parallel with the public value echoed in the public sector. The integration of corporate social responsibility (CSR) in the business model addresses public interest and public value. However, corporate activities that seek to promote public interest and values are limited and tainted with business-motivated efforts. Moreover, these activities are basically an extension of self-interest and tend to maximize benefits through image making. Still, economic values are the main thing for the private organization.

The apparent difference in terms of vision, strategy and main values distinct to both private and public organizations, plainly suggests that their operating systems are not the same. One can surely observe, for example, the organizational characteristics that describe public organization such as environments, cultures, structures, processes, and people are different from that of the private organization.

Discussion Questions on Agency Case

1   Why do you think public organizations are prone to criticism?

2   From your perspective, which criticisms of the public sector are warranted? Are private companies more or less prone to criticism? Why or why not?

3   How might the study of organization theory and public management help the public manager who is interested in improving the perception of her agency?

4   Discuss some of the challenges to effective public management and the reform of public organizations.

5   How do you think the image of the public sector has changed in the past five years? Have you personally experienced any improvements in public service delivery? If yes, what are these improvements and why did they happen? If no, why do think this was the case?

6   Does ownership matter – i.e. does the efficiency or effectiveness of a service dependon whether it is in the public or private sector? Why? How would you collectevidence to support your view – and how would you collect evidence to try to refuteit?

Class Exercises

1   In groups, identify the main differences between 'public management' and 'privatemanagement'. Thinking about the news over the past month, identify instances where these concepts might help in deciding who has been responsible for things which have been going wrong in your area or in your country (Now try answering the question in terms of things which have been going right in your area or your country).

2   In groups, identify some public services in your area which are provided by private sector firms. Each group should identify ways in which these services are less 'public' than those which are provided by the public sector. Then compare your answers in a plenary session.

2. Research Notes

Research Note 1

Driven to Service
: Intrinsic and Extrinsic Motivation for
Public and Nonprofit Managers

This research draws upon a survey of nonprofit and state government managers to examine the role service motivation plays in both sectors. The research addresses three main research questions: 1) What are the main motivational dimensions and constructs of managers in the public and nonprofit sectors? 2) How are these different types of work motivations related to each other? and 3) What differences exist between these sectors in terms of level of intrinsic and extrinsic work motivation? Our findings suggest there are four different motivational constructs and in many ways public and nonprofit managers are similar in terms of the importance of intrinsic rather than extrinsic motivation. While the mean level of extrinsic motivation in the public sector is statistically higher than in the nonprofit sector, certain types of extrinsic motivation such as advancement motivation and WLB motivation are highly correlated with intrinsic motivation in both the public and nonprofit sectors. Finally, directions for future research and practical implications are also discussed.

Research Framework

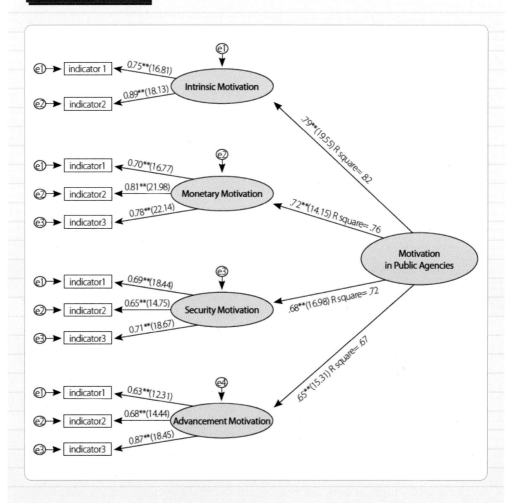

Research Framework

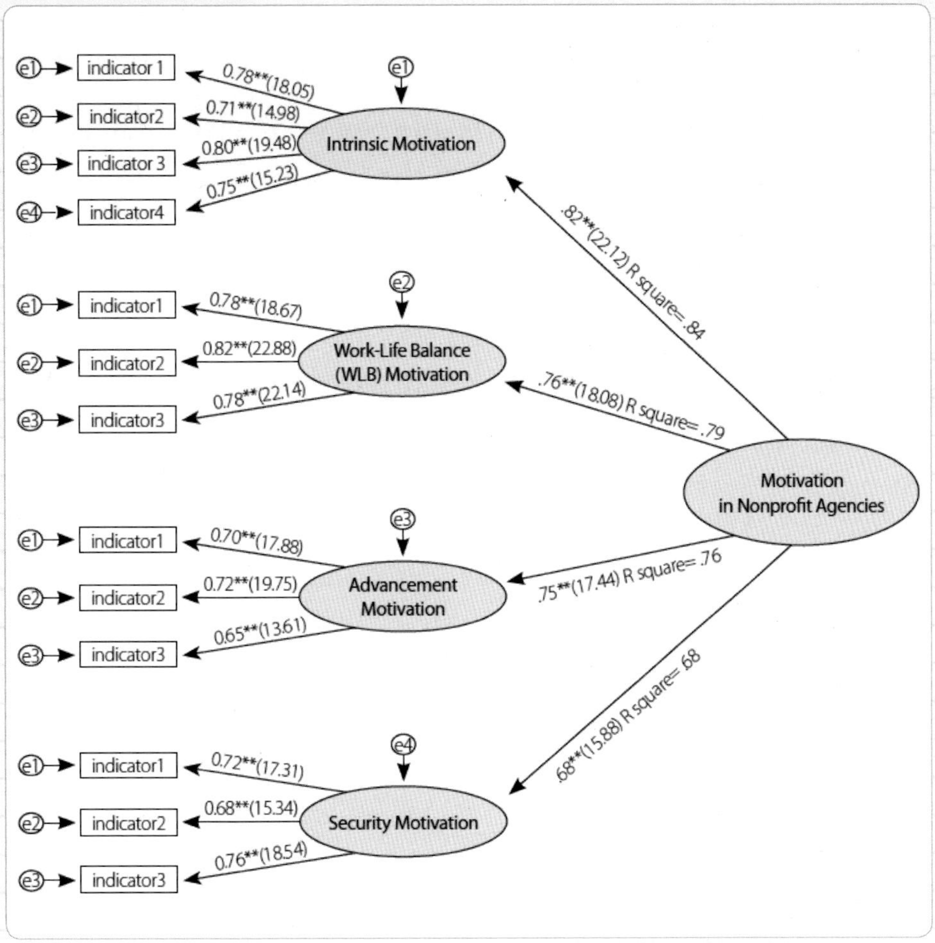

Source: Park & Word (2012)

Serving the Mission
: Organizational Antecedents and Social Consequences of Job Choice Motivation in the Nonprofit Sector

Competition for employee talent is important to the success of any organization, including those in the nonprofit sector. This research examines the motivational and demographic characteristics of nonprofit managers in order to gain a better understanding of these managers that may ultimately inform both practice and theory. This research examines 1) job choice motivation, 2) intrinsic and extrinsic motivation, and 3) demographic and organizational factors affecting individuals working for the nonprofit sector. Subsequently, our model proposes that job choice motivation comprises intrinsic motivation and three types of extrinsic motivation, and examines the organizational antecedents and social outcomes of motivation to work in the nonprofit sector. The findings suggest that individuals who work in the nonprofit sector are intrinsically motivated in terms of job choice. Furthermore, personal characteristics such as gender, age, ethnicity, type of job, and level of education impact both job choice motivation and the level of intrinsic motivation.

Research Framework

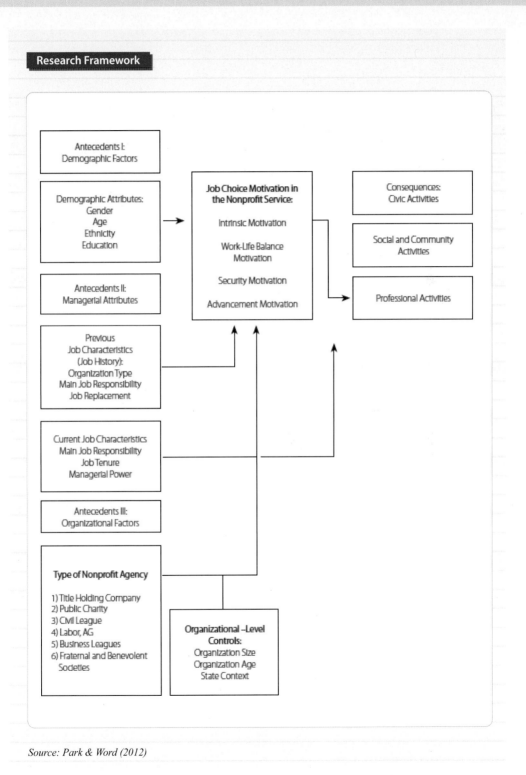

Source: Park & Word (2012)

Environments

Framework

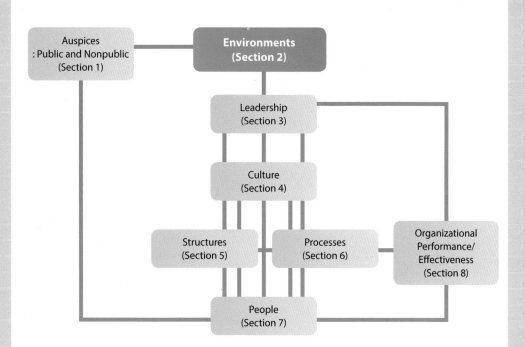

Source: Park, S. M. (2013). *Public Management: A Research Handbook*.
Daeyoung Moonhwasa Publishing Company.

Keyword

- External Environments
- Legal Conditions
- Political Conditions
- Economic Conditions
- Ecological Conditions
- Cultural Conditions
- Technological Conditions
- Demographic Conditions
- Mechanistic Form
- Contingency Theory

- Mechanistic Form
- Organic Form
- Capacity
- Homogeneity & Heterogeneity
- Stability & Instability
- Concentration & Dispersion
- Turbulence
- Munificence
- Complexity
- Dynamism

Role Play Simulation

1

1. Play One's Role as a Public Administrator

Disgruntled Volunteers

In a suburban county outside a large city, the Parks and Recreation Department has been run for decades by a friendly, popular director who has run the volunteer program for the department by himself. He had a network of friends throughout the county that served as volunteer coaches, as teachers in recreational programs (art, music, dance, exercise), and in other roles. In turn, these volunteers drew in other volunteers to serve as timers, scorers, and assistants, and in the other necessary roles. The director loved working with this network of friends that he had developed over the years, and the volunteer program virtually ran itself, with the director's administrative assistant simply filling a roster with the names of people who called in, chatted with the director, and then chose a role.

The director has now retired, after a large banquet with numerous warm testimonials and expressions of appreciation. The new director is younger and new to the county. The county commissioners and county administrator hired her in part out of respect for her administrative training (a master's degree and various training programs) and administrative skills that she displayed in her previous position as assistant director in the Parks and Recreation department of a medium-sized city. They have asked her to work on shaping up the department's budgeting and financial procedures, its communications and accountability to the commission and the county administrator's office, and its internal organization.

Several of them have quietly mentioned to her that as much as they loved the former director, "Old Ed" was wonderful but wanted to do things his way, and "it was hard to know what was going on over there sometimes." The county was under increasing financial pressure, and it would be harder and harder to grant the budget increases that Old Ed asked for, especially without the popular support he could always bring to help the commissioners justify the increase. In addition, auditors were becoming increasingly critical of the budgets and accounts of the department. No one suspected any wrongdoing, but organization and management clearly needed improvement.

The new director feels concerned about the loose organization of the volunteer program. Drawing on some of the policies at her previous organization, she initiates the requirement that volunteers will need to sign a waiver of liability, and to sign statements that they will follow a drug-free policy and avoid sexual harassment. She also begins considering setting up a training program for volunteers, through the National Youth Sports Coaches Association, and may ask the coaches to pay for their training. The word of these changes and possible changes spreads rapidly among the volunteers.

In getting to work on her various priorities, the new director finds the constant phone calls from volunteers to be too disruptive to her other work. Knowing that it is not a satisfactory long-term solution, she asks her administrative assistant to handle the conversations and assignments of the volunteers himself, as best he can. Within two weeks, problems arise. Soccer season is starting, and there is a shortage of coaches for the first time ever. The new director asks the administrative assistant to find more volunteers to serve as coaches. The assistant finds a few. He also reports back that some former coaches are refusing, saying they get the sense that their contributions are not really valued, and without Old Ed as center of the activity, it is just not the same any more. Some comment that the new requirements imply distrust and are demeaning, and involve too much red tape. The new director has to stop all other activity, get on the phone, and talk some of these reluctant volunteers into continuing. She shores up the soccer program for the time being. Some of these old-timers tell her that the problem will get worse when t-ball and baseball season starts. She also hears that the exercise and dance instructors have told the administrative assistant that they may not continue.

The new director has called in your group to assist her in improving the volunteer program. She asks that you advise her on what to do about the volunteers. She can only offer you a small consulting fee and lunch, but you have agreed to try to help because you are so good-hearted and professional.

Source: The case was written by Dr. Hal G. Rainey

Warm-Up Questions

1　Where does the new director stand now? What are the first questions you would ask about her current situation, or the first key observations, that are pertinent to assessing her volunteer program and what should be done with it? Please list at least five key points or questions. Be able to discuss how these points relate to concepts and frameworks covered in the course.

2　What should the new director do? What are key points and priorities for a well-managed volunteer program? What conditions, arrangements, policies, and procedures should she definitely try to establish? Please list at least five key points or priorities. Discuss how these relate to concepts and frameworks covered in the course.

3　How does the case reflect the challenges of managing in a public sector context?

4　What should other authorities do to help her? What could other levels of administration and government do to support her volunteer efforts?

Source: The discussion questions were based on the case written by Dr. Hal G. Rainey

2. Play One's Role as a Government Reformer

Let's suppose you are the chairman of a private firm called, Government Organizational Planning and Analysis (GOPA) based in Korea. Main services of your company are the identification of different factors that affects government performance; establish coping strategies with the inevitable changes surrounding the public organizations; and offer environmental scanning for public organizations. The email below is a letter from the Minister of the Ministry of Public Management requesting your company for consultancy and the development of a reform strategy applicable for the Ministry of Security and Public Administration (MOSPA). Please read the email and let's try to determine possible actions to address their request.

From	Minister Sup-Jong Cho (minsiter_mpm@korea.com) You moved this message to its current location.
Sent	Thursday, May 21, 2014 3:34:29 PM
To	Tae-Yong Lee (gopachairman@gopa.com)

3 attachment | Download all as zip (1802.0 KB) Intention Letter.docx (568.0 KB) Request for Environmental Scanning & MOSPA's Strategic Reorganization Plan_mpm.docx (698.0 KB) Park to Disband Coast Guard.docx (536.0 KB)

View online

TAE-YONG LEE, Ph.D.
Chairman,
GOPA, Korea

Dear Dr. Lee,

Your company, Government Organizational Planning and Analysis (GOPA) has long been a government partner in improving the capacity of public agencies in delivering services for the citizens. The annual publication of your Asian Public Sector Performance Analysis and Environmental Scanning for public organizations are useful materials that educate public managers; and I confess I am a regular subscriber of those journals.

Anyway, let me go directly to my purpose. You are aware for sure that our government was bombarded with left-to-right criticisms on the MV Sewol tragic incident and the public demands government's responsibility of such unacceptable failure. It is really hard to admit but the government's emergency management systems is flawed and manifestly inefficient, thus in a way have exposed the deeply-rooted problems in our bureaucracy.

President Park made a public announcement that a major government revamp will be expected and initially identified two major government agencies to undergo radical reform, the Ministry of Security and Public Administration (MOSPA) and the Korea Coast Guard (KCG).

As the country's government agency entrusted with the formulation of a comprehensive reform plan, we are in the process of developing a strategic reorganization plan for MOSPA and soon to be submitted to the President. Along with this, our office is also trying to identify issues, specifically external environmental changes that affect the general performance of MOSPA; and suggest effective measures to deal with such environmental challenges.

Considering your company's tract record, we would like to engage your services to assists us in the (1) Drafting of a MOSPA's Strategic Reorganization Plan, and (2) Environmental Scanning for MOSPA that will include problems and external environment challenges faced by the agency.

Thank you very much and hoping for a successful collaboration with your company.

Truly yours,

Sup-Jong Cho
Minister,
Ministry of Public Management

Attached File 1: Problem-Based Learning (PBL)

Request for Environmental Scanning & MOSPA's Strategic Reorganization Plan

	Step	Contents		
1	Environments/ Conditions/ Backgrounds	Please explain the situation briefly.		
2	Problem Definition	In your own perspective, please be as specific as possible when pointing out the problem.		
3	Actual Case Studies	Please explain by giving specific examples (Newspaper articles, news clips, or Interviews)		
4	Finding Alternatives	**Possible Solutions**	**Merits/Pros in a Korean Context**	**Demerits/Cons in a Korean Context**
		①		
		②		
		③		
5	The Best Solution	Why did you choose this alternative as the best solution? What are the expected effects and potential contribution?		

 **Attached File 2**

Park to Disband Coast Guard

Tearful president takes full responsibility, vows public safety reforms

... The president in a nationally televised address said she would carry out a series of sweeping reforms to improve the country's safety standards and erect a new state emergency system to prevent further disasters like the Sewol ferry sinking.

As part of her drastic reform measures, Park said she would disband the Coast Guard for its failed rescue mission and execute extensive reorganizations of the Ministry of Security and Public Administration and the Ministry of Maritime Affairs and Fisheries for their failures in handling and preventing the disaster. ...

... The president said the Coast Guard's rescue efforts failed, and all of its functions would be transferred to other agencies including the new Ministry of National Safety that she previously proposed.

"(The Coast Guard's) functions of investigation and intelligence will be transferred to the National Police Agency, and its roles of rescue operations and maritime security will be moved to the new ministry of national safety to greatly reinforce the professionalism and responsibility over maritime safety," she said.

The Coast Guard has come under scrutiny for its poor initial response that it could have saved more lives if officials had made more rescue efforts as the ferry was sinking. The president also lashed out at the related ministries of security and maritime affairs, saying they have also failed to protect the lives of the people. Their key roles will be turning to the new ministries to be launched under the Prime Minister's Office. ...

*Source: The information contained in this article was extracted from
"The Korea Herald (2014.05.19)" by Chung-un Cho*

2 Theory Synopsis

Nowadays, public organizations exist in an unstable environment due to various organizational challenges brought by inevitable environmental changes. Berry (2007) noticed that, as public sector organizations seek to improve performance, effectiveness, and accountability; they face the challenges of environment brought by managerial, political, and technical changes. Section 2 focuses on the emergence of external environment factors as a public management concept and its growing influence in public governance. External environment factors are outside the scope of public organizational management, but they commonly affect organizational effectiveness, organizational behavior, decision making, and management process.

External environment factors are represented by different conditions in the organization management, including political, economic, cultural, and technological. These conditions are vital issues both for private and public sector organization. Nevertheless, they are more important in public management because of the distinct characteristics of the public sector as elaborated in section 1 of this book. This section briefly explores different external environment factors, their importance, conceptual, and theoretical background that will explain their relationship with environment and management.

1. Types of External Environment Factor

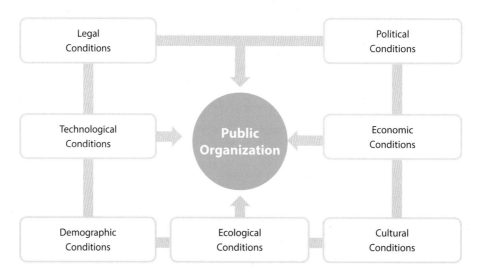

External Environment Factors

Source: Rainey (2014)

1) Legal Condition

**Rainey
(2014, p.88)**

Laws, regulations, legal procedures, court decisions; characteristics of legal institutions and values, such as provisions for individual character- istics of legal institutions and values, such as provisions for individual rights and jury trials as well as the general institutionalization and stabili- ty of legal processes.

2) Political Conditions

**Rainey
(2014, p.88)**

Characteristics of the political processes and institutions in a society, such as the general form of government (socialism, communism, capitalism, and so on; degree of centralization, fragmentation, or federalism) and the degree of political stability (Carroll, Delacroix, & Goodstein, 1988). More direct and specific conditions include electoral outcomes, political party alignments and success, and policy initiatives within regimes.

3) Economic Conditions

Rainey
(2014, p.88)

Levels of prosperity, inflation, interest rates, and tax rates; characteristics of labor, capital, and economic markets within and between nations.

4) Cultural Conditions

Rainey
(2014, p.88)

Predominant values, attitudes, beliefs, social customs, and socialization processes concerning such things as sex roles, family structure, work orientation, and religious and political practices.

5) Technological Conditions

Rainey
(2014, p.88)

The general level of knowledge and capability in science, engineering, medicine, and other substantive areas; general capacities for communication, transportation, information processing, medical services, military weaponry, environmental analysis, production and manufacturing processes, and agricultural production.

6) Ecological Conditions

Rainey
(2014, p.88)

Characteristics of the physical environment, including climate, geographical characteristics, pollution, natural resources, and the nature and density of organizational populations.

7) Demographic Conditions

**Rainey
(2014, p.88)**

Characteristics of the population such as age, gender, race, religion, and ethnic categories.

2. The Importance of External Environment Factor

External Environment

Diversity and complexity
in the public administration
are increasing rapidly.

**Public
Management**

Publicness and politically
are reflected in the public
management.

Environmental influences
play a crucial role
in institutionalization processes
in organization.

Source: Rainey (2014, pp. 90-94)

3. Analytical Dimensions of Environments

1) Aldrich (1979)'s Point of View

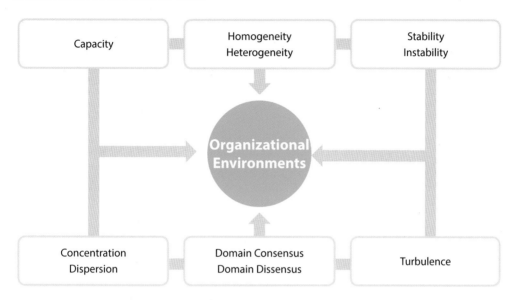

Source: Aldrich (1979), Rainey (2014, p. 93)

① Capacity

The extent to which the environment affords a rich or lean supply of necessary resources.

Source: Aldrich (1979), Rainey (2014, p. 93)

② Homogeneity / Heterogeneity

The degree to which important components of the environment are similar or dissimilar.

Source: Aldrich (1979), Rainey (2014, p. 93)

③ Stability / Instability

Aldrich (1979)

The degree and rapidity of change in the important components or processes in the environment.

Source: Aldrich (1979), Rainey (2014, p. 93)

④ Concentration / Dispersion

Aldrich (1979)

The degree to which important components of the environment are separated or close together, geographically or in terms of communication or logistics.

Source: Aldrich (1979), Rainey (2014, p. 93)

⑤ Domain Consensus / Domain Dissensus

Aldrich (1979)

The degree to which the organization's domain (its operating locations, major functions and activities, and clients and customers served) is generally accepted or disputed and contested.

Source: Aldrich (1979), Rainey (2014, p. 93)

⑥ Turbulence

Aldrich (1979)

The degree to which changes in one part or aspect of the environment in turn create changes in another; the tendency of changes to reverberate and spread.

Source: Aldrich (1979), Rainey (2014, p. 93)

2) Dess & Beard (1984)'s Point of View

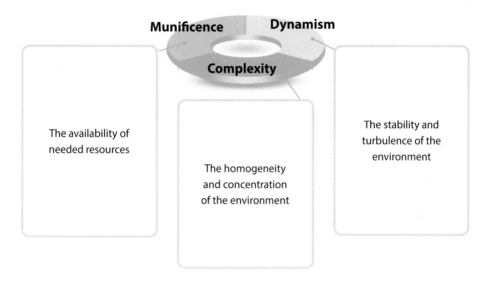

Source: Dess & Beard (1984), Rainey (2014, p. 93)

3. Mechanistic Forms vs. Organic Forms

Mechanistic	Organic
• Tasks are separated	• Employee contribution to shared tasks
• Tasks are narrowly defined hierarchy with centralized top down	• Teamwork redefines tasks
• Control rules are pervasive	• Flatter with less hierarchy
• Communication is vertical	• Fewer rule
	• Knowledge and control of tasks are located anywhere in the organization
	• Communication is horizontal

1) Mechanistic Form - Stable Conditions

Burns & Stalker (1961)

Stable conditions suggest the use of a mechanistic form with tradition-al patterns of hierarchy, reliance on formal rules and regulations, vertical communication, and structured decision making.

2) Organic Forms - Dynamic Condition

Burns & Stalker (1961)

More dynamic conditions – situations with a rapid changing environ-ment – require an organic form which is less rigid, more participative, and relies on workers to redefine their positions and relationships.

4. Contingency Theory

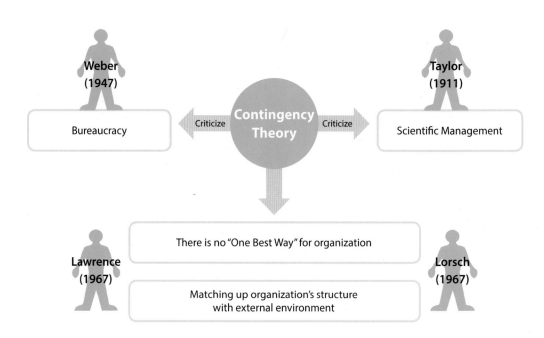

Weber (1947)

Taylor (1911)

Bureaucracy

Criticize   **Contingency Theory**   Criticize

Scientific Management

Lawrence (1967)

There is no "One Best Way" for organization

Matching up organization's structure with external environment

Lorsch (1967)

Lawrence & Lorsch (1967)

Lawrence and Lorsch (1967) studied firms in three industries whose environments exhibited difference degrees of **uncertainty** as a result of more or less rapid changes and greater or lesser **complexity.**

As changes in the environment became more rapid and frequent, and as the environment became more complex, these conditions imposed more uncertainty on decision makers in the organizations.

Lawrence & Lorsch (1967)

Lawrence & Lorsch (1967)

The most successful firms had structures with a degree of complexity **matching** that of the environment.

Organizations in more stables environments could manage with relative traditional, hierarchical structures. Organizations in more unstable, un-certain environments could not.

Lawrence & Lorsch (1967)

Rainey (2014, p. 91)

Organizations must adopt structures that are as complex as the environ-ments they confront.

An Organization's structure must be adapted to environmental contin-gencies as well as other contingencies.

Rainey (2014, p. 92)

Rainey (2014, p. 92)

In simple, homogeneous, stable environments, organizations can successfully adopt mechanistic and centralized structure.

In more complex and unstable environments, successful organizations must be organic and decentralized, partitioned into many departments with correspondingly elaborate integrating processes.

Rainey (2014, p. 91)

Source: Lawrence & Lorsh (1967), Rainey (2014, pp. 91-92)

From Theory to Practice

1. Agency Analysis

National Police Agency

Employing the different classifications of environment, we will try to deal with the issues and challenges besetting the National Police Agency (NPA) of Korea. The following are the five classifications of environment: 1) demographic environments; 2) technical environment; 3) political environment; 4) legal environment; and 5) office environment. Interviewing a senior police officer, we will identify possible problems in each classifications of environment and determine course of actions that may address issue(s) or problem(s) in the police organization.

External Environments of NPA

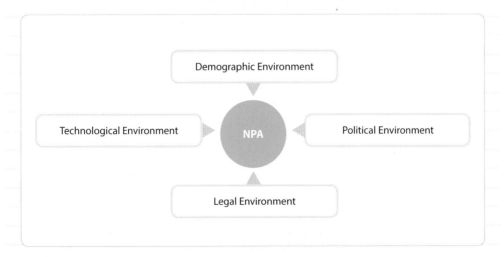

1) Demographic Environment

In a globalized and multicultural society, demographic environment is a very important element that is worth consideration. Nowadays, there is an enormous integration of Korean citizens to various racial and cultural orientations from different countries. Many Koreans go abroad for business, studying, travel, and in some cases immigrate to other country (there were about 7 million Koreans as of 2013[MOFAT, 2013]). Along with this, the Korean society has been hosting millions of foreign nationals who are students, foreign workers, marriage immigrants, tourists, industrial trainees, businessman, among others. In 2013, number of foreigners living in Korea surpassed 1.45 million accounting 2.8% of the country's total population—Chinese residents being the largest foreign group (53.7%), Vietnamese (12.2%), Americans (4.8%), and Filipinos (4%), respectively (Yonhap News Agency, 2013).

At any rate, and because of the growing number of foreign residents in Korea, foreigner perpetrated crimes have extremely increased in a faster rate. In a report released by Korean Institute of Criminology, the number of arrested foreign criminal suspects nearly doubled from 14,524 in 2007 to 27,144 in 2011 (Yonhap News Agency, 2013) . Murder, rape, arson, robbery, and drug related crimes are among the criminal offenses implicated against foreigners (see Korea Times, 2012). Albeit the increasing rate of crime allegedly committed by foreigners, an impartial and fair investigation is more important than ever. Advocating for a crime-free society must be in accord with the principles of justice and human rights. Like other perpetrators, suspected foreign criminals must be afforded due process of law and respect of human rights. In an interview with a police officer on the environmental changes brought by the increasing number of foreigners, it was revealed that in dealing with suspected foreign criminal, police investigations and interrogations are aided with a language interpreter to ensure understanding of the nature of the offense imputed against a foreigner. Sometimes police officers use online web service which could interpret and translate conversations during lawful interrogations of apprehended foreign suspected criminals. This online service was developed by the Ministry of Culture, the Ministry of Foreign Affairs and the Korean National Police.

However, the available services in the police organization can't completely assume gargantuan responsibility of ensuring impartial, fair, and effective disposition of a case that involves foreign national. For example, the online web service has a lot of limitations in the protection of substantive as well as procedural rights of a foreigner under custody or interrogation. Though online services can address simple conversations, an in-depth and complex interrogations of extracting facts of a crime cannot be perfectly translated by a mere computer-aided intervention. Any lapses or misinterpretation of any single information can compromise the fate of a foreign suspect. The limited number of Korean police officers even raised a question on their capability in dealing with the increasing foreigner perpetrated crimes and ensuring safety of other foreign residents. In a data published by the government, it was revealed that one Korean police officer is responsible for 501 citizens (Korea Times, 2013) .

The role of the police organization in the effective integration of citizens and foreign residents in a multicultural society is critical. The maintenance of peace and order requires an evenhanded enforcement of the law; observance and satisfaction of due process; and recognition of fundamental rights of every human being—citizen or non-citizen. Giving an emphasis for foreign residents, the police organization must endeavor to bridge the communication gap through effective means. Meaning, there should be more manpower that are language experts that understand or speak diverse languages. Also, through research and development, the police organization can determine specific police functions that can effectively utilize online web interpretation and translation service.

2) Technological Environment

Korea is one of the leading countries on information technology (IT) and the world's leader in internet connectivity (Pingdom, 2013). Along with the advancement of technology and high-speed ICT infrastructure, new types of cybercrimes—crimes through network and computer—emerged and soared up to a great extent. For the effective enforcement of laws, the extension of criminal activities in the "cyber space" that widened the scope and breadth of criminal activitynecessitates the adoption of effective counter-measures. With the demands of the environmental changes brought by ICT and technological advancements, Korean National Police Agency (KNPA) seriously meted strategies to deal with cyber criminals. The results of the interview with the police officer revealed that training and education on cybercrime is carried out by a special educational institution. Police officers who wish to work on cybercrime unit are required to complete a curriculum of 110 hours; and at odd times, they must learn through online lecture materials, at their own pace anytime and in anyplace. After the completion of the training and education program, police officers are assigned to a cyber-investigation team (squad).

The scope of environmental changes warrants skillful and technical savvy police officers to curb crimes committed through the cyber zone. Besides the effort to train and educate police officers, the agency recruits highly qualified and experienced professionals as civilian experts to enhance the capacity of the cybercrime investigation unit. Recently, however, the police agency decided to elevate the cyber-investigation team from "국" (guk) to "과" (gwa). It means that the police force is capable of independently producing cybercrime experts within their ranks.

Drawing from the initiatives of the Korea National Police Agency (KNPA), one may think on the worthiness of the adopted organizational measures to counter cyber criminals. The complexity of addressing cybercrimes and threats demands a deployment of knowledgeable cyber sheriffs. The short-term training and education program seems to be lacking and may raise doubts on its capacity to increase efficiency of a police officer assigned in a cybercrime investigation. The short-term program may not be able to produce experts that can fully understand the technical complexities of internet crimes. Cybercrime experts are computer security specialists—computer experts and digital forensics professionals. Thus, the police agency can adopt a detailed human resource development (HRD) programor establish an agency policy that can best address the issue.

The adoption of a self-paced learning system can be helpful; however, this must not be treated as a stand-alone learning approach. The integration of monitoring and evaluation of learning process can help the participants effectively manage learning.

Lastly, the need for special employment of civilian experts may help reinforce the needed knowledge, skills, and abilities in the police agency's cybercrime unit. Like other criminal investigation units, the cyber-investigation bureau should be maintained and developed through a long-term perspective. As every citizens of the world are nearly wired and connected through internet, the role of police in the future will be more diverse and complex.

3) Political Environment

The political influence takes various forms, and its careful understanding depends on the leadership thrusts and directions. In every political campaign, candidates present their platform of governance and promise various reforms for the interest of the public. Upon assumption to office the candidate-elect will initiate reforms in accordance with the platform of government. President Geun-Hye Park, for example, emphasizes the eradication of what she perceived four social evils, which includes: 1) sexual violence; 2) family violence; 3) school violence; and 4) unsanitary food. In this regard, we cannot fail to note that Park administration's main thrust of government is the promotion of people's welfare, safety, and security. Interestingly, President Park initiates changes even in the names of agencies. The Ministry of Public Administration and Security was changed to Ministry of Security and Public Administration to give priority on people's safety and security. However, turns of events made the Park's administration to rename again the agency into Ministry of Government Administration and Home Affairs, it's original name from 1998 to 2008 (Korea Joongang Daily, 2014).

In line with the administration's thrusts of government, the police agency must determine courses of actions in order to achieve the visions and objectives of the president—eradication of four social evils. In the interview, the police officer mentioned that there will be an increase in the number of police force. President Park promised that an additional 20,000 new police recruits will be included in the agency in five years. These new recruits will be deployed in the police stations, substations, and in the police constabulary. However, the delivery of the promised new recruits is yet to come. The police agency has to stretch the available manpower to attend to various security and safety efforts for the citizen in the midst of an ever-expanding breadth of role in the society. Thus, one may just conclude that work efficiency can easily compromise and affects the morale of the whole police ranks.

Indeed, political impact can disturb police agencies' thrusts and direction in a given period of time. For example, efforts on coping with the political demands results to resource maneuvering, reshuffling, and organizational re-orientation. This calls for a flexible police organization that can easily cope with whatever political changes. Piecemeal initiatives from different political orientations may influence the organization but responses must not appear to be an overhaul of the agency's system. Changes in the political environment are usual occurrence. Thus, an expected and abrupt coping measure must always be in place.

4) Legal Environment

As a police officer, their main job is the maintenance of peace and order through the enforcement and application of law. Generally, statutes and laws by nature are coercive, thus considered the main weapon of police officers on going against violators, criminals, or offenders. In the Korean context, besides the special laws and applicable statutes, police officers are guided by the doctrines and principles of laws laid in the Korean criminal law, which defines felonies or crimes, requisites, and penalties involved. Recently, however, the growing number of violent crimes—sexual assault, assault, bullying, negligence, harassment, and domestic violence—put the "Law on the Punishment of Violent Acts" in the limelight.

The letter of the law that details the criminal liability and penalty may appear ideal to every Koreans; laws may be good but it appears there are problems and issues on its effective enforcement and application. Among others, the capability of the Korean police officers as law enforcers are tainted with doubts for they lack the legal knowledge on handling cases. Police officers don't have to be a legal expert or a lawyer to be abreast of the legal doctrines, but the nature of their duty requires them to practice and understand heartily the letters and interpretation of laws.

Discussion Questions on Agency Case

1   Using a nonprofit entity and a public agency as examples, prepare a memo describing the general environmental conditions of both organizations. Describe the technological, legal, political, economic, ecological, and cultural conditions.

2   Choose a public agency or department and describe the ways in which societal values and institutions influence its operation.

3   At present, what is the main cause of 'market failure' in your country? Which state interventions are most likely to correct it in a cost-effective way?

4   At present, what is the main cause of 'government failure' in your country? Which market-based solutions are most likely to correct this government failure in acost-effective way?

5   Interview an official or an elected politician who is responsible for public sector reforms at national or local levels in your country. You might ask:

- What do you perceive as the key challenges facing public agencies at present?
- How do you respond to these changes?
- What are the lessons to be learned from past reforms?

6   Check out the public sector reform programme of another OECD country on the OECD website (www.oecd.org/gov) and compare it with the reform agenda of your own country. Where do you see differences and commonalities?

Class Exercises

Mapping the reform paths of public sector reforms in your country, work as a team with other students on this task:

1 Research sources in the library, on the Internet (in particular OECD) on the public sector reforms in your country and try to identify major reform themes.

2 Discuss what you have identified and try to agree on the three main reform themes in your country.

3 Divide these three themes between three teams. Each team should identify the evolution of the reform process in respect with that theme. This involves:

   - Identifying different phases of the reform process (with changing priorities);
   - Description of the main reform objectives of each phase; discussing what has been achieved and what the problems were.

4 Present this outline to your fellow students in the other teams and discuss whether or not the identified reform paths have been consistent.

2. Research Notes

Research Note 1

Of Alternating Waves and Shifting Shores
: The Configuration of Reform Values
in the US Federal Bureaucracy

Scholars have noted that United States federal government reforms come in waves (Barley & Kunda, 1992; Kettl, 2002; Light, 1998), often accompanied by values that alternate between rational and normative conceptions of public administration and service. The idea of alternation also suggests the importance of time in gauging the effect of new reforms when previous reforms have accumulated from the past (see Pollitt, 2008). Time is a necessary variable in implementing reforms; time is crucial to know if reform values have taken hold. Extending Paul Light's (1998) reform waves metaphor, we investigate here whether two predominant management philosophies have influenced and reconfigured the shoreline of values found among federal agencies over a particular period of time. Using empirical methods, we examine how the values of New Public Management and its humanist (post-NPM) counterpart have settled and taken hold among US federal agencies. We followed three lines of inquiry: determining the existence of reform values in the bureaucracy, examining the prevalence of different sets of values, and investigating whether 'crowding out' of values occurred, that is, whether there was a detectable shift in the distribution of values as a new wave came on top of others. Our analysis yields evidence for the predominance of certain NPM and post-NPM values and indicates that bureaucracy concurrently holds what may be regarded as competing values side-by-side. Implications for research and future reforms are suggested in the final section of the article.

Research Framework

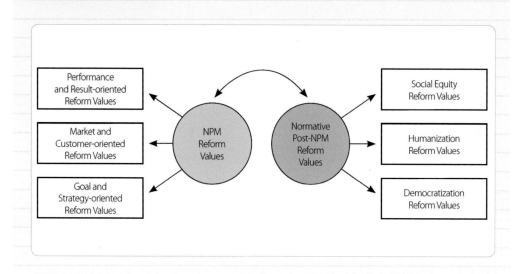

Source: Park & Joaquin (2012)

Research Note 2

Analyzing Value Creation of
Electronic Human Resource Management (E-HRM)
: An Indonesian Case

Information and communication technologies (ICT) advancement, coupled with an ever-increasing demand for the human resource management (HRM) function to be more efficient, effective, and capable of supporting the strategic goals of every business function, has led to the adoption of electronic human resource management (e-HRM). This study aims to provide both insight and empirical evidence on the success enabler of e-HRM acceptance and e-HRM value creation in the public sector. The study confirms that perceived usefulness (PU) is found to be a strong predictor of e-HRM usage. From an organizational and managerial standpoint, HRM strength has a positive influence on e-HRM usage. In the creation of HRM values, we find e-HRM usage to be a strong predictor of perceived human resource (HR) service quality but not a predictor of the creation of a strategic role for the HRM function. Furthermore, the study indicates that HRM strength is an important direct predictor of the creation of HRM values. Hence, this relationship suggests the importance of policy clarity and consistency. To ensure that e-HRM is used in a more strategic way, the core business functions of an organization, HRM strategy and IT management, should be clearly aligned and integrated. A set of theoretical and practical implications as well as the limitations of this research are also discussed.

Research Framework

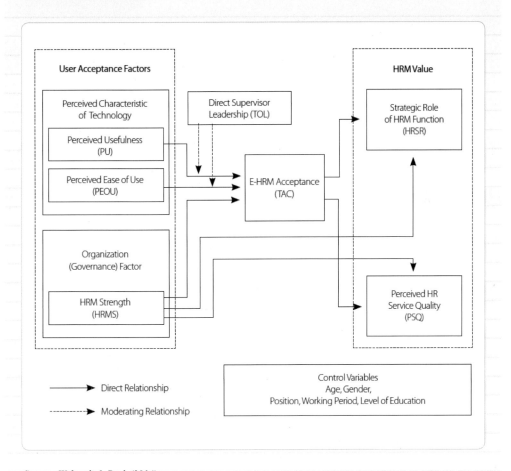

Source: Wahyudi & Park (2014)

Leadership

Framework

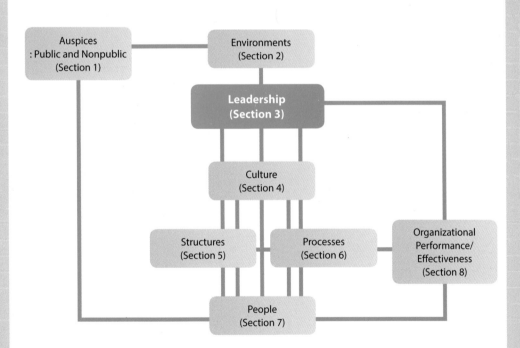

Source: Park, S. M. (2013). *Public Management: A Research Handbook*.
Daeyoung Moonhwasa Publishing Company.

Keyword

- □ Leadership
- □ Leadership Capacity
- □ Trait Theory
- □ Behavior Theory
- □ Situational Theory
- □ The Ohio State Leadership Studies
- □ Managerial Grid
- □ Contingency Theory
- □ Situational Theory
- □ Path-Goal Theory

- □ Transactional Leadership
- □ Transformational Leadership
- □ Servant Leadership
- □ Ethical Leadership
- □ Leader-Member Exchange Theory

① Role Play Simulation

1. Play One's Role as a Public Administrator

A Funeral in the Public Service Center

For many years, the Social Security Administration (SSA) followed a very bureaucratized process for handling claims. A "claim" is a request for services, such as a retiree's application for SSA to begin paying his or her social security benefits (that is, to start sending monthly checks to him or her). Claims handling also involves many different functions, such as updating records, adding and deleting dependents and relatives from records, handling changes in the requests, and other matters.

For years, the claims would be handled like this: a client (a citizen making a claim) would apply at a local Social Security Administration office, or by mail. The local office would forward the claim to one of eight public service centers (PSCs) in eight different regions of the country. At the PSC, a different unit would handle each different phase of handling the claim. One unit would receive the claim and route it to the others. Another unit had specialists, called claims authorizers, who would rule on the legality of the claim—did the person have a legitimate claim? Then a claim would be shipped, with a large batch of other claims, to a next unit that contained benefits authorizers, or specialists who would calculate how much the client should receive in social security payments. Then the claim would move to another unit for disbursement or payment of claims, and to another for filing and retention. This process was like a big assembly line, with the claim moving from one phase of the work to another.

Congress added many programs and specifications to social security and related programs. At the same time, the nation's population grew and became more complex. The claims-handling process got much more complicated, and this assembly-line system began to have problems, such as many delays in handling claims and many lost claims. As an example of the problems with the system, when a benefits authorizer would find that a claims authorizer had not provided all the information about a claim that the benefits authorizer needed, the claim had to be delivered back to the claims authorization unit that had previously handled it. Often, the returned claim went back to a different person from the one who worked on it to begin with. This resulted in slow processing and frequent mistakes.

SSA went through a long period of trying to figure out how to resolve the problems, and finally decided to adopt a modular design in the PSCs. They put together in units, called modules, all the different specialists needed to process a claim—claims authorizers, benefits authorizers, typists, file clerks, and others. These groups worked together like teams. They would take a client's claim and work it through to completion, so that they actually had the person as the client of their module—they could identify the clients as theirs. They could also communicate more readily with each other about any problems that came up. There were some tough problems in implementing this new system, but it worked out very well, and has become the standard design in the PSCs.

Time passes and brings changes that require adjustments by all people and organizations. Advances in information technology—computers and communications technology—brought changes for the SSA. The processing of claims became more computerized. Local offices handle many claims by entering the data directly into the main SSA computers in Baltimore, and getting answers back directly. This reduced the load of claims coming to the PSCs. In addition, the work in the PSCs became more computerized and automated through higher technologies. Claims authorizers and benefits authorizers handled more correspondence by simply hitting a key on the computer terminal that caused the needed correspondence to print out. This reduced the need for typists. More information was going directly into the computer, and requiring less paperwork, and this reduced the need for file clerks to file the papers. The modules needed fewer and fewer typists and file clerks. This created problems, because if a module needed only a couple of file clerks, and was only assigned two, the module became more dependent upon their work habits. If both file clerks were absent, the module managers had to do the filing to keep the module's work going.

Social Relations Among Specialists. In the old system, a social and educational hierarchy existed among the specialists. Benefits authorizers were the most highly paid and highly trained, followed by claims authorizers, and then by typists and filing clerks. The filing clerks were often single mothers with low incomes and low educational levels. They often struggled with serious personal challenges in their lives outside of work. They would sometimes miss work or arrive late because of child care problems. When SSA moved to the modules, the move helped to break down social distance between these groups. The file clerks would work directly with the others, usually as friends and coworkers. Also, SSA tried to move file clerks up the ranks through training and development processes.

In one of the PSCs in the midwestern United States, the assistant director (A.D.) of the PSC had an idea for responding to the problem of the declining need for file clerks. He started a new organizational design, in which file clerks were assigned to special units, from which they would be farmed out, as needed, to the modules. The design was something like the old idea of a typing pool or secretarial pool. The problem was that the file clerks felt isolated and demoted by being taken out of their modules.

The A.D. learned of the file clerks' unhappiness in a fairly dramatic way. In his office one day, he received a request from the members of the file clerks' unit to come down to their office area. When he arrived, he found the office draped with black crepe and black balloons. A large black casket lay on a desk in the middle of the room. The file clerks, dressed in funeral clothing, began singing funeral hymns. A spokesperson for the group came forward to tell him that they were there to hold a funeral for the file clerks unit, to mourn the death of the file clerks.

The A.D. was stunned. He had heard that the file clerks were unhappy with the change he had made, but had not expected such a development. He was not sure how to proceed. He was not really sure what the "funeral" was supposed to mean or to communicate, except that the file clerks were unhappy. Questions were running through his mind. What should he do right now, as he faced the file clerks and their funeral? What should he do in the longer term? Should he discipline them? He knew that people in other units would be very aware of how he treated these file clerks and some would complain if he "let them get away" with such disruption and insubordination. Because of the problems mentioned earlier, that file clerks often had with late arrival or absences, the discipline and work habits of the file clerks were sensitive issues in the PSC.

Source: The case was written by Dr. Hal G. Rainey

Warm-Up Questions

1   Analyze the incident in relation to questions of values.

    - What values was the A.D. promoting with the change?
    - What values were the file clerks emphasizing through their behavior?

2   What motivation concepts and theories help you to analyze the case?

3   What leadership concepts and theories help you to analyze the case?

4   On the basis of your answers to the preceding questions, make suggestions
    to the A.D. about actions he should take.

    - What should he say and do, as he stands before the file clerks at their
      "funeral?"
    - Once he leaves the room and returns to his office, what should he plan to
      do in the longer term?
    - In advising him on actions to take, try to express the relations between
      your advice and important issues about values, motivation, and leadership.

Source: The discussion questions were based on the case written by Dr. Hal G. Rainey

2. Play One's Role as a Government Reformer

Let's suppose you are the manager of Human Resource Development Strategy Office under the Ministry of Public Management in Korea. The Minister sent a memorandum via email directing your office to develop a leadership program for the ministry. Please read the memorandum for the whole details of the directives and let's try to comply with the order of the Minister

From Minister Sup-Jong Cho (minsiter_mpm@korea.com) You moved this message to its current location.

Sent Monday, May 22, 20153:34:29 PM

To HRD Strategy Office (hrdso_mpm@korea.com)

2 attachment | Download all as zip (1234.0 KB) Plan for Leadership Development Program.docx (698.0 KB) CEO Leadership Needed in Public Office.docx (536.0 KB)

View online

MEMORANDUM-MPM0002

TO: The Manager, Human Resource Development Strategy Office (HRDSO)
RE: Leadership Development Program
FROM: The Minister, Ministry of Public Management
DATE: 22May 2014

- -

We must be aware that leadership and management strategies in the public sector are not permanent. Leaders must always be aware with the growing organizational challenges and employ appropriate leadership approach. Among the emerging new types of public sector leadership is the CEO type and entrepreneurship.

As the Minister, I saw the importance and relevance of enhancing our leadership capabilities by learning various leadership styles and strategies. It is through learning that we may be able to grasp the organizational circumstances and effectively adopt leadership and managerial attitudes.

In connection hereof, I am directing your good office to develop a "Plan for Leadership Development Program" that will focus on training and educating our people with the values and principles of emerging types of leadership—CEO and entrepreneurship. Upon completion, you are hereby required to submit the final concept of the program to my office. I would like you to give a serious attention and provide an elaborate response(s) on the following issues:

a. What are the key challenges facing public sector leadership in Korea?
b. What factors might cause leadership failure?
c. What is the best way to develop public sector leadership capacity and nurture excellent leadership?
d. Please propose specific alternatives, options, and solutions, especially from entrepreneurial viewpoints.

For your immediate action and compliance.

Attached File 1: Problem-Based Learning (PBL)

Plan for Leadership Development Program

	Step	Contents		
1	Environments/ Conditions/ Backgrounds	Please explain the situation briefly.		
2	Problem Definition	In your own perspective, please be as specific as possible when pointing out the problem.		
3	Actual Case Studies	Please explain by giving specific examples (Newspaper articles, news clips, or Interviews)		
4	Finding Alternatives	Possible Solutions	Merits/Pros in a Korean Context	Demerits/Cons in a Korean Context
		①		
		②		
		③		
5	The Best Solution	Why did you choose this alternative as the best solution? What are the expected effects and potential contribution?		

Attached File 2

CEO Leadership Needed in Public Office

... Bureaucrats, on the other hand, are often defensive players who generally see the world in terms of positions held constant or lost within the greater context of a fixed (not positive) sum game. Bureaucrats allocate their time and resources to maintain their fixed slices of pie, and that one person`s larger slice is seen as the result of another person`s smaller slice (a "my gain is your loss" mentality). Most bureaucrats therefore play the management game (albeit of a city, province, state, or country) much like one-dimensional chess, spending scarce resources trying to put the opponent`s king piece in checkmate to declare so-called "victory," usually relating to a politically-based proposition or initiative. The problem is that such behavior often ends in stalemate (congressional gridlock, or in extreme cases, the actual shutting down of government, as seen in the U.S. Congress in the mid-1990s); this is not too different from World War I-type positional trench warfare in which small bits of territory went back and forth, with needless casualties and lost precious resources.

Until recently, the CEO and bureaucratic worlds rarely intersected. The thinking was that the two areas were "apples and oranges," in which the perception was that the skill set of one could not be leveraged to the other. This is no longer the case in today`s globalized world. CEOs have now decided to leverage a successful career in terms of wealth creation beyond the corporate world to make a more meaningful impact on society. Many CEOs are intelligent, driven, and answer to the ultimate client, their shareholders. If you think about it, these same traits and drive to satisfy the client is not too dissimilar to what`s needed to be a successful bureaucrat, especially when one equates answering to shareholders as answering to a political constituency. Viewed this way, the "apples and oranges" quickly converge to "apples and apples," which allows many CEOs to add value outside the boardroom. ...

Source: The information contained in this article was extracted from
"The Korea Herald (2005.10.25)" by Jasper S. Kim

2 Theory Synopsis

Leadership in the public sector is an important aspect of employee's work environment. Effective public sector leaders possess some major characteristics of value-based leadership styles;that is, directive leadership, transformational and transactional leadership, charismatic and servant leadership, and empowering and integrated leadership. The recent literature also demonstrates that organizational leadership can be analyzed based on a hierarchical spectrum in the organizations. That is, leadership behaviors vary among different levels of management and supervisory and managerial status, for example, vertical or top-down leadership and distributed or shared team-based leadership. Organizational leaders must strive to maximize the performance and job satisfaction of their subordinates in order to achieve organizational goals. Indeed, leadership can be defined as "a process whereby an individual influences a group of individuals" to attain common goals by mobilizing and motivating the workforce (Northouse, 2004, 3).

Effective leadership provides "cohesiveness, personal development, and higher levels of satisfaction," and gives a sense of "direction and vision, an alignment with the environment, a healthy mechanism for innovation and creativity, and a resource for invigorating the organizational culture" (Van Wart 2003, 214). Increasingly prominent in leadership research are the concepts of transformational and transactional leadership, servant and ethical theory, and leader-member exchange theory. Section 3 provides an overview of the leadership theories, practices, cases, and implications. This section also introduces and explores sets of leadership cases in Korean public agencies to bridge the gap between theories and practices as well as to generalize the aforementioned leadership theories into other cultural settings.

1. The Concept of Leadership

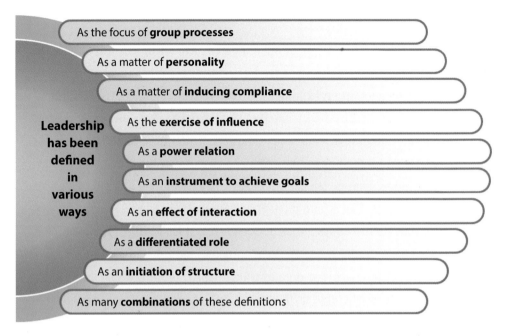

Leadership has been defined in various ways

- As the focus of **group processes**
- As a matter of **personality**
- As a matter of **inducing compliance**
- As the **exercise of influence**
- As a **power relation**
- As an **instrument to achieve goals**
- As an **effect of interaction**
- As a **differentiated role**
- As an **initiation of structure**
- As many **combinations** of these definitions

Source: Bass (1997)

Rainey (2014, p. 337)

By leadership, most people mean the capacity of someone to direct and energize people to achieve goals.

Leadership can be defined as "a process whereby an individual influences a group of individuals" to attain common goals... by mobilizing and motivation the workforce.

Northouse (2004, p. 3)

Robbins & Judge (2011, p. 410)

The ability to influence a group toward the achievement of a vision or set of goals.

Leadership is the process of developing ideas and a vision, living by values that support those ideas and that vision, influencing others to embrace them in their own behaviors, and making hard decisions about human and other resources.

Slocum & Hellriegel (2011, p. 4)

2. Theory of Leadership

1) Trait Theories

Robbins & Judge (2011, p. 411)

Theories that consider personal qualities and characteristics that differentiate leaders form nonleaders.

The traits model of leadership is based on characteristics of many leaders—both successful and unsuccessful—and is used to predict leadership effectiveness.

Slocum & Hellriegel (2011, p. 299)

2) Behavioral Theories of Leadership

Robbins & Judge (2011, p. 415)

Theories proposing that specific behaviors differentiate leaders from non-leaders

The behavioral model of leadership focuses on what leaders actually do and how they do it

Slocum & Hellriegel (2011, p. 302)

① The Ohio State Leadership Studies

Consideration

Consideration refers to a leader's concern for his or her relationships with subordinates

Initiating structure refers to a leader's emphasis on setting standards, assigning roles, and pressing for productivity and performance

Initiating Structure

Source: Rainey (2014, pp. 337-338)

② The Blake and Mouton Managerial Grid

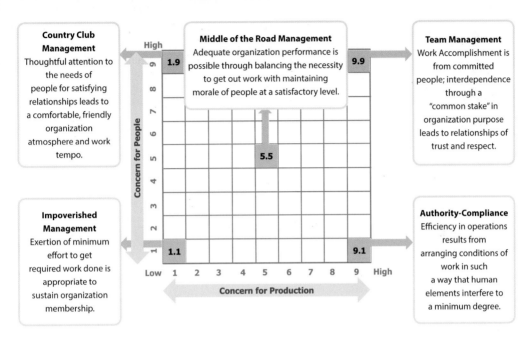

Source: Blake & McCanse (1991)

3) Contingency Theories

① Fiedler's Contingency Theory

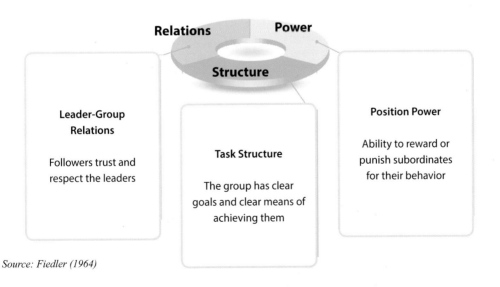

Source: Fiedler (1964)

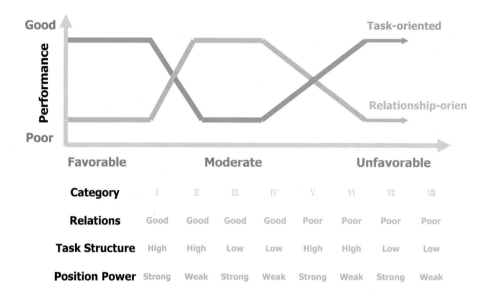

Category	I	II	III	IV	V	VI	VII	VIII
Relations	Good	Good	Good	Good	Poor	Poor	Poor	Poor
Task Structure	High	High	Low	Low	High	High	Low	Low
Position Power	Strong	Weak	Strong	Weak	Strong	Weak	Strong	Weak

Source: Fiedler et al. (1977)

② The Path-Goal Theory of Leadership

Directive Leadership

Enhances satisfaction and expectancies
If the task is ambiguous, but hurts them
If the task is well structured and clear.

Supportive Leadership

Enhances satisfaction when tasks are
frustrating and stressful,
but can be inappropriate when the task,
the work group, and the organization
provide plenty of encouragement.

Leadership

Achievement-oriented Leadership

Increases performance on ambiguous tasks,
either because those conditions allow
ambitious goals more often than simple tasks do,
or because achievement-oriented
subordinates tend to select such tasks.

Participative Leadership

Works for best for ambiguous tasks in which
subordinates feel that their self-esteem is
at stake, because participation allows them to
influence decisions and work out solutions.

Source: Rainey (2014, p. 341)

4) Transactional Leadership

Contingent Reward

Leaders engage in a constructive path goal transaction of reward for performance. They clarify expectations, exchange promises and resources for support of the leaders, arrange mutually satisfactory agreements, negotiate for resources, exchange assistance for effort, and provide commendations for successful follower performance.

Active Management by Exception

Leaders monitor followers' performance and take corrective action if deviations from standards occur. They enforce rules to avoid mistakes.

Transactional Leadership

Passive Management by Exception

Leaders fail to intervene until problems become serious. They wait to take action until mistakes are brought to their attention.

Laissez-Fair Leadership

Leaders avoid accepting their responsibilities, are absent when needed, fail to follow up requests for assistance, and resist expressing their views on important issues.

Source: Bass (1997, p. 134)

5) Transformational Leadership

Inspirational Motivation

Leaders articulate an appealing vision of the future, challenge followers with high standards, talk optimistically with enthusiasm, and provide encouragement and meaning for what needs to be done.

Intellectual Stimulation

Leaders question old assumptions, traditions, and beliefs; stimulate in others new perspectives and ways of doing things; and encourage the expression of ideas and reasons.

Transformational Leadership

Idealized Influence

Leaders display conviction; Emphasize trust; take stands on difficult issues; present their most important values; and emphasize the importance of purpose, commitment, and the ethical consequences of decisions.

Individualized Consideration

Leaders deal with others as individuals; consider their individual needs, abilities, and aspirations; listen attentively; further their development; advise; teach; and coach.

Source: Bass (1997, p. 133)

111

6) Servant Leadership

Greenleaf (2008)

The servant-leader is servant first... Becoming a servant-leader begins with the natural feeling that one wants to serve, to serve first. Then conscious choice brings one to aspire to lead. That person is sharply different from one who is leader first, perhaps because of the need to assuage an unusual power drive or to acquire material possessions. For such people, it will be a later choice to serve—after leadership is established. The leader-first and the servant-first are two extreme types. Between them are the shadings and blends that are part of the infinite variety of human nature.

Source: Greenleaf (2008)

Listening	Conceptualization
Empathy	Foresight
Healing	**Servant Leadership**	Stewardship
Awareness	Commitment to the Growth of People
Persuasion	Building Community

Source: Spear (2010)

7) Ethical Leadership

Brown & Trevino (2002)

The demonstration of normatively appropriate conduct through personal actions and interpersonal relationships, and the promotion of such conduct to followers through two-way communication, reinforcement, and decision-making.

8) Leader-Member Exchange Theory

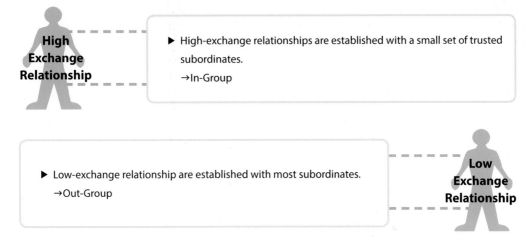

Source: Rainey (2014, p. 344)

3. The Coming Wave

From Theory to Practice

1. Agency Analysis

Korea Electric Power Corporation (KEPCO)

KEPCO is a Korean-based public enterprise[1], incorporated on 1982 and was recognized as a juridical person through the Korea Electric Power Corporation Act[2]. The company is mandated to stabilize and sustain electric supply and meet the electric power demands of the citizen. From its incorporation, the company continuously explores electric power resources, generates, transmits, transforms, and distributes electricity all over the country.

In spite of being a public enterprise, the company endeavors to improve and increase its efficiency. For example in 2001, the company was separated into 6 power plants introducing competition system in the production department. The company is also preparing for the separation of sales department. KEPCO is now moving towards global market; the company is striving to provide sustainable and prompt electric power supply based on outstanding electric power quality.

Notwithstanding the company's success on its various business segments,

---

1 KEPCO is classified as a market-oriented public corporation defined under Management of Public Institutions Act of Korea.

2 The Korea Electric Power Corporation Act was enacted to provide a legal mandate for the enhancement and stabilization of electric supply in Korea. The law was first passed through Act No. 4903 (March 26, 1989) and was subsequently amended thrice – through Act No. 4541 (March 6, 1993), Act No. 5573 (Sept. 23, 1998), and Act No. 6755 (Dec. 5, 2002), respectively. Article 1 of the said law states, "The purpose of this Korea Electric Power Corporation Act (the "Act") is to enhance stabilization of supply of electric power by promoting development of power resources and ensuring the reasonable operation of electricity business through establishment of the Korea Electric Power Corporation, and further to contribute to the development of the national economy."

there are issues that impede the maximization of organizational gains such as the company's leadership approach. Concomitantly, KEPCO employee's job satisfaction is considerably low which raises serious concern for the whole organization. Thus, in this section we will try to determine the prevailing leadership approaches in KEPCO and relate it with job satisfaction.

1) Transactional Leadership

Transactional leadership is a leadership style in which subordinate employees performs tasks through negotiated efforts or through both rewards and punishment. As a leadership model, the relationship between leaders and subordinates are based on a pattern of negotiated transaction and compliance. Transactional leaders are extrinsic motivators and effective negotiators for behavioral compliance. They use rewards and punishment systems to motivate employees within an organization with predetermined goals, established structure and culture. Bass (1997) identified two important components of transactional leadership; (1) conditional rewards, and (2) management-by-exception.

□ Conditional Rewards

In a conditional reward (also known as contingent reward), transactional leaders provide a determining mechanism for rewards and punishments (Bass, 1990). Basically, an agreement is drawn between the leader and subordinate rewarding efforts and recognizing good performance. They both determine what must be done to be rewarded and what are to be avoided in order not to get punishment. After the agreement, leaders and subordinates accept the mutual role and responsibility for the decided goals. Leaders provide subordinates either reward or punishment in the case of goal achievement.

□ **Management by Exception**

Managementbyexception means that leader only interfere when subordinates fail to reach an acceptable performance level and show some undesirable behaviors that deviate from the standards. Leaders in a management by exception engage in searching and correcting misbehaviors. They enforce policies and specific rules to avoid mistakes (Bass, 1997). Management by exception can either be active or passive. Leaders in an active management by exception immediately intervene when signs of behavioral deviation appear. Leaders in a passive management by exception intervene only when mistakes causes serious and bad results. One of the popular critics on management by exception is on the timing of leader's intervention on unwanted employee behavior. Leaders interfere only when subordinates committed mistakes, thus a belated leadership reaction.

An in-depth leadership analysis employed in KEPCO, it appears that the company adheres to the principles and practices laid in the transactional leadership. The table below shows the specific company measures that explains its adherence to the two types of transactional leadership behaviors – contingent reward and management by exception (i.e., passive and active).

Transactional Leadership Behavior in KEPCO

Contingent Reward	Contingent Reward	Passive Management by Exception
Incentive system is in place; employees are rewarded based on their performance.	Training and education system is in place. Employees undergo training and education to learn all necessary KSAs for the performance of tasks.	Consumer feedback mechanism is in place. After providing services to their consumers, they ask customers to give their feedback on the company's service delivery. Based on the feedbacks, KEPCO reeducate under performing employees.

2) Blake and Mouton's Managerial Grid

The Managerial Grid Model (Blake and Mouton, 1964) characterizes organization's leadership style based on two dimensions: concern for people and concern for production. In the grid, concern for people falls on the x-axis, while concern for production in the y-axis; each axis ranges from 1-9 (low-high). The managerial grid theory identified five different leadership styles: (1) impoverished management, (2) country club management, (3) authority-compliance, (4) middle of the road Management, and (5) team management. Blake and Mouton presume team management as the leader's paramount behavior.

Graphical Representation of Blake and Mouton's Managerial Grid

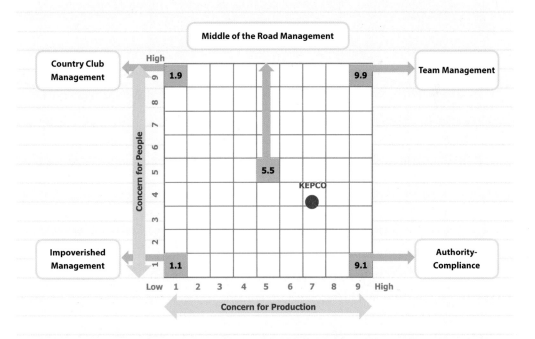

In a survey questionnaire conducted in the company, it reveals that concern for production (6.8) is higher than concern for people (3.7). The result implies that

KEPCO's leadership style falls close to authority-compliance in the Blake and Mouton's managerial grid.

3) KEPCO's Leadership and the Need for New Leadership Approach

The KEPCO's leadership analysis proved an adherence with thetransactional leadership behaviors and a concurrence with the Blake and Mouton's Managerial Grid Model. As a public enterprise, the company must be responsive towards national development. The transactional leadership behavior tends to direct employees and lead them towards the achievement of a national call for responsiveness towards development. The action-oriented transactional leaders carry with them strong behavioral tendency of task management.

However, despite the company's success on its various business segment, the company fails to address important issues confronting their employees. For example, employees who are working at the KEPCO's help desk are suffering from lots of stress because of the wicked civil complaints and customer service. Undeniably, the company is doing remarkable effortsin the improvement of customer's satisfaction level. The irony, however, organizational measures that will help employees to cope from serious mental and physical stresses are not present. One can easily assume that, the company lacks individual consideration and is concern mainly on organizational output.

Transactional leadership can address organizational issues through employees that are extrinsically motivated, however, only in a short period of time. There is a need for the adoption of a leadership style which can trigger subordinate's intrinsic motivation in a hierarchical organizational structure. Servant leadership may best address the leadership issues in KEPCO.

□ Servant Leadership

Servant leadership can address the prevailing organizational management issues in KEPCO. Servant leadership can most likely depict the characteristics of a participative leadership. Subordinate employees are respected and trusted by leader; and have a positive relationship with leader. Leaders display caring and encouraging leadership behavior that shows concern to the personal and emotional needs of the employees. The positive relationship between the leader and subordinates results to a sense of normative reciprocal obligation to work in accordance with the leader's direction. In other words, servant leadership is capable of boosting subordinates' trust in the leadership and organization.

Discussion Questions on Agency Case

1 As a leader, how would you direct your organization that is undergoing significant change? In your answer, recall the discussion on the KEPCO agency case in this chapter.

2 Discuss transformational and charismatic leadership styles. Can you identify these leadership behaviors in Korean public sector?

3 Please also compare transformational behaviors and transactional behaviors. Do you think these leadership styles are dependent on the organizational culture and structure? Which leadership behaviors could be more effective to improve and enhance public employees' work motivation in a way that helps achieve organizational goals?

4 Interview two organizational leaders, one in the private, and one in the public sector. You might ask:

- Do you see yourself as a leader or as a manager?
- How would you describe the responsibility of being a leader?
- What do people expect of you as a leader?

5 Can you deduce any differences between public and private sector leadership?

Class Exercises

Work as a team with three other students on this three-part task:

1   Research sources in the library, and find an article or paper which reports on some recent studies on organizational leadership. Your chosen study should have been carried out no earlier than year 2000.

2   Write a summary of this study.

3   Present your summary to your colleague students. Include in your presentation something about what you have learned about your own leadership approaches and styles as you carried out this exercise.

2. Research Notes

Research Note 1

Leadership and Public Service Motivation in U.S. Federal Agencies

This analysis of over 6,900 federal employees' responses to the Merit Principles Survey 2000 examines the influences of leadership and motivational variables, and especially public service motivation, on the "outcome" variables job satisfaction, perceived performance, quality of work, and turnover intentions. CFA confirms a factor structure for transformation-oriented leadership (TOL), public service-oriented motivation (PSOM), transaction-oriented leadership (TSOL), and extrinsically oriented motivation (EOM). Multivariate regression analysis shows that TOL and PSOM, as well as interaction effects of TOL-TSOL and TOL-PSOM, have strong relations to the outcome variables. SEM analysis examines direct and indirect effects of the main variables. Overall, the results indicate that TOL and PSOM have more positive relations to the outcome variables than do TSOL and EOM. The combination of high TOL and high PSOM has the strongest positive, and hence desirable, relation with organizational outcomes. Among this very large sample of federal employees, those who perceived their leader as displaying TOL (i.e., leadership that is encouraging, supportive, informative, and that emphasizes high standards) also expressed higher levels of PSOM and higher levels of job satisfaction, perceived performance and work quality, and lower turnover intentions. The SEM analysis further indicates that TOL has these effects by way of empowerment, goal clarification, and PSOM, and is distinct from TSOL (transactionoriented) leadership, which shows no such relationships.

Research Framework

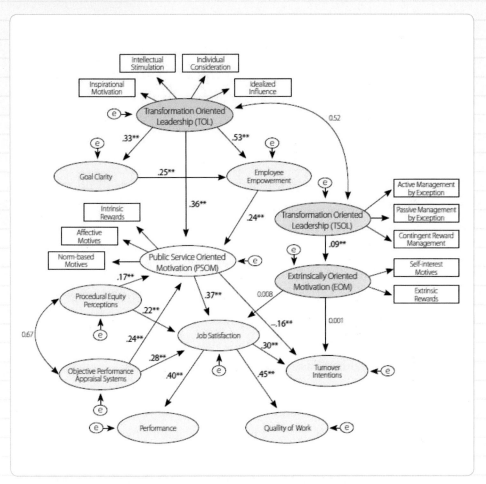

Source: Park & Rainey (2008)

Toward the Trusted Public Organization
: Untangling the Leadership, Motivation,
and Trust Relationship
in U.S. Federal Agencies

The purpose of this study is to probe the main determinants of organizational trust, as identified in the relevant literature: cognition-based (i.e., rational) trust and affect-based (i.e., relational) trust. This study explores the nature of trust among public employees and identifies important antecedents and moderating conditions based on systematic and rigorous empirical research. Using large data sets from Merit Principles Survey (MPS) and Best Places to Work (BPTW), as well as drawing upon the scholarly works from several disciplines, this study develops an antecedent-trust model and analyzes the different types of antecedents of organizational trust in the public sector at a hierarchical and multilevel ordering structure. The focus of the study is empirically testing the effects of vertical and shared leadership behaviors and work motivation attributes on organizational trust within U.S. federal agencies. In addition, the moderating impact of leadership on the relationship between work motivation and organizational trust is examined. This research finds that some of these predictors and moderators (e.g., vertical and shared leadership behaviors) play significant roles in fostering organizational trust directly and indirectly. Based on a discussion of the main findings, research and practical implications for public management theory and practice are provided.

Research Framework

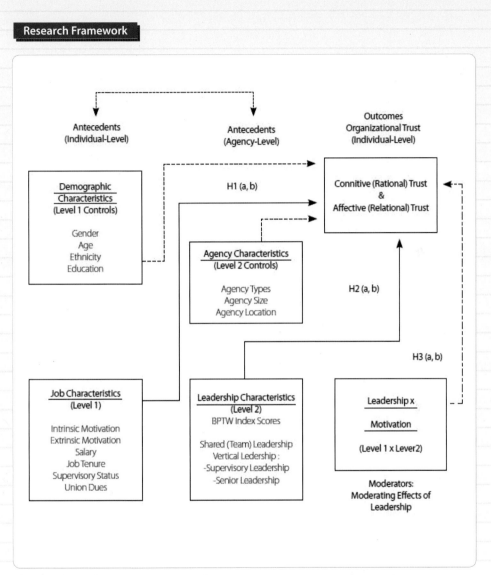

Source: Park (2012)

Culture

Framework

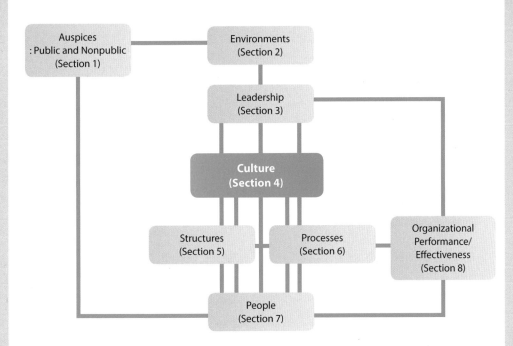

Source: Park, S. M. (2013). *Public Management: A Research Handbook*.
        Daeyoung Moonhwasa Publishing Company.

Keyword

- Organizational Culture
- Power Distance
- Uncertainty Avoidance
- Individualism
- Collectivism
- Gender Role Orientation
- Masculinity
- Femininity
- Long-term Orientation
- Short-term Orientation

- Group Culture
- Developmental Culture
- Hierarchical Culture
- Rational Culture
- Competing Value Framework
- Clan Form
- Adhocracy Form
- Hierarchy Form
- Market Form
- Globe Studies

Role Play Simulation

1. Play One's Role as a Public Administrator

Crummy Contract

The new director described in the "vanishing volunteers" case has also received another charge from the county administrator and commissioners. Due to budgetary pressures and tax resistance, the county must emphasize financial stringency. Two new county commissioners have just been elected after campaigns emphasizing that they would seek to cut the county's budget and find more efficient ways of managing programs and departments. Among other proposals, they are calling for more "privatization" and "contracting-out" to improve the efficiency of county operations. They and others have emphasized this priority in discussions with the new Parks and Recreation director.

These pressures already existed before the new director and new commissioners arrived, and the former commissioner had responded to some degree. He had contracted with a local operator of fast food franchises to take over the food concessions at the three county parks and two county recreation centers. The county had previously operated these food service outlets, but normally broke even on them. The new operator contracted to run them and pay the county a small fee. When the contract was let, the former director told the commissioners that this fee would allow the county to actually make a little money instead of breaking even on the food concessions.

The contract is coming up for renewal soon. The new director receives word that one of the concessions in one of the parks has essentially shut down. They are only offering candy and cokes and similar food items, and not the hot dogs,

129

hamburgers, and cooked items that they had previously offered. The contractor informs the new director that the stoves and refrigerator have broken down, and that the county must repair them for the cooked food service to resume. The contract did not specify who was to be responsible for maintaining the equipment, and the operator is arguing that it is the county's responsibility. The expenses involved in performing the maintenance will erase the county's small gain through the fee from the contractor.

In addition, the new director is receiving reports of complaints about the quality of the food, and of accumulating litter and trash near the food service outlets. In talks with the contractor, she finds that he takes the position that cleanliness outside the food service outlets is not his responsibility. He says she needs to assign more maintenance personnel to clean up.

Some people have called to complain that they used to plan picnics based on using the food from the outlets, but the food and service had deteriorated and they would not do so any longer. The new director increasingly forms the impression that the contractor, experienced in running fast food franchises supervised and supported by national corporations, was not prepared for some of the new conditions in the county food services (for example, no central supply of foods and other supplies, or central support on equipment maintenance). From her conversations with the contractor, she worries that he may renege on the fee to the county, since he has hinted that if he loses money he does not have to pay the fee. The contract is loosely drawn, and she intends to talk to the county attorney about whether the contractor could get away with this action. The county attorney is also a private contractor with the county, and is not very responsive to requests for his time. Talking with the attorney, moreover, will not really solve the problem. Even if the food services contractor did not have sound legal grounds, she is loathe to get into a legal and public dispute with him, since he is a prominent local businessman with connections to the new county administrators and other members of the business community.

In addition to these headaches with food services, the new director finds that the two new county commissioners and some of their friends in the business community are leading a push for more privatization. They have issued a policy statement from their Association of Brilliantly Efficient and Effective Business Entrepreneurs that calls for such steps, and their association president has appeared at a county commission meeting to promote the report and its main priorities. The statement asserts that county business organizations can provide services more efficiently and effectively than government-operated services, and that government operation of services that local businesses could perform represents unfair competition. Lauding the successful privatization of some county food services activities, they call for further initiatives in such areas as grounds maintenance, equipment maintenance and operation, and the operation of other facilities such as parks, swimming pools, and recreation centers. The county has a putt-putt golf range at one of the parks and the report specifically targets that activity for privatization.

Again, the new director finds that the county's contracting process has been run rather informally and personally by the beloved former director. There is no evidence of any illegality, but the process needs better management.

Again, also, your group, good-hearted professional public servants that you are, has agreed to serve as a poorly compensated advisory group to try to help out a fellow professional and public servant.

Source: The case was written by Dr. Hal G. Rainey

Warm-Up Questions

1   What does the new director know or need to know? Prepare a list of key questions or points of information about the current situation that you and she need to consider, in assessing the current situation and preparing a response to it. Please list at least five key questions or points and explain how they relate to ideas and concepts covered in the course.

2   Where does the new director need to go? What should she strive to achieve, in the organization and processes for contracting in the department? What conditions, arrangements, policies, and procedures should she definitely try to establish? Please list at least five priorities and explain how they relate to matters covered in the course.

3   How does the case involve the implications of managing in a public sector environment?

4   What could other levels of government and authority do to support her management of privatization and contracting?

Source: The discussion questions were based on the case written by Dr. Hal G. Rainey

2. Play One's Role as a Government Reformer

Let's suppose you are the Minister of the Ministry of Public Management in Korea. In view of the reorganization and impending changes in the government, the Prime Minister sent an email addressed to you as the Minister asking for the expertise of your office to look into the possibility of an organizational cultural reform. Below is the full text of the email; read and let's discuss what are the possible measures and course of actions to be adopted in order to satisfy the order of the Prime Minister.

From Prime Minister Jong-ManLee (primeministerkorea.com) You moved this message to its current location.

Sent Monday, May 28, 2014 10:34:29 AM

To Minister Sup-Jong Cho (minsiter_mpm@korea.com)

3 attachment | Download all as zip (1802.0 KB) Intention Letter.docx (568.0 KB) Request for Culture Reform Plan_mpm.docx (698.0 KB) Foreign Interns Face Office Culture Shock .docx (536.0 KB)

View online

SUP-JONG CHO

Minister,

Ministry of Public Management, Korea

Dear Minister Cho,

From the words of President Guen-Hye Park, there were still issues and problems that are drawing back our public organization and bureaucracy. It may not be the exact words of the President; however, she seems to imply the public agencies' backward culture and practices as the main culprit of government inefficiency.

I know it clearly that starting an organizational cultural change is a gigantic task that requires radical and progressive approach. With faith in your ministry, I would like you to look into the possibility of adopting cultural reform strategies for our public organization and the bureaucracy. I urge you to submit a 'cultural reform memorandum' that will detail your determined plan of action. In this project, we wish the following issues must be addressed:

It is believed that the Korean public personnel systems, norms, and practices have been deeply influenced in many ways by the Confucian cultural legacies, such as collectivism, ritualism (or formalism), and hierarchical harmonization.

a. What do you think are the main cultural factors that might lead to negative outcomes in Korean bureaucracy?
b. Do you think the "Gwanfia" cultures and practices deeply rooted in Korean bureaucracy?
c. If so, can you propose a set of possible sweeping measures aimed at fixing these problems rampant in the public sector?

I know MPM can play a key role in this endeavor for our country and our people.

Truly yours,

Jong-Man Lee
Prime Minister
Republic of Korea

Attached File 1: Problem-Based Learning (PBL)

Request for Culture Reform Plan

	Step	Contents		
1	Environments/ Conditions/ Backgrounds	Please explain the situation briefly.		
2	Problem Definition	In your own perspective, please be as specific as possible when pointing out the problem.		
3	Actual Case Studies	Please explain by giving specific examples (Newspaper articles, news clips, or Interviews)		
4	Finding Alternatives		Possible Solutions	Merits/Pros in a Korean Context	Demerits/Cons in a Korean Context
		①			
		②			
		③			
5	The Best Solution	Why did you choose this alternative as the best solution? What are the expected effects and potential contribution?		

135

Attached File 2

Foreign Interns Face Office Culture Shock

Foreign student interns at Seoul Museum of Art say
rigid hierarchy is biggest sticking point

For foreigners joining the Korean workforce for the first time, addressing seniors and coworkers properly can be a major challenge. That is how Liu Jing, 24, from China and Mary Tarakey, 24, from Switzerland felt when they started interning at the Seoul Museum of Art headquarters.

"It was really difficult to adjust to this kind of working atmosphere. There is a strict hierarchy between seonbaes (seniors) and hubaes (juniors), so you have to make sure to adjust properly to those who are above your position," said Tarakey, a senior undergraduate student at Hanyang University. "It is very difficult for me." ...

... "Something I still struggle with is figuring out what to call my seniors. Since I don't know everyone's titles or positions, I would just refer to everyone as 'teacher' in hopes of showing respect towards anyone and everyone," said Liu, a graduate student majoring in Korean language and literature at Yonsei University.

In Korea, hierarchy is the defining basis of relationships, particularly in the workplace where one's authority rises with position and age. Therefore, addressing someone by his or her job title or position is important because title indicates status. If seniors are not addressed by juniors in a way that fits his or her position, the senior may feel offended. ...

... "Even greeting people is difficult because we meet them several times a day and don't know whether to bow or greet them every time or not," Liu said. "I think the internship is good training for a future job here." Liu majored in Korean during her undergraduate studies in China before coming to Seoul two years ago to further study the Korean language and culture. She hopes to work here upon graduation.

Source: The information contained in this article was extracted from
"The Korea Herald (2014.02.02)" by Ji-Young Sohn

2 Theory Synopsis

Section 4 deals with the topic of organizational culture and other related issues. Many researchers and practitioners posit that certain types of organizational cultures have either positive or negative outcomes vis-à-vis either the effectiveness of the organization or for individual employees within the organization. Organizational culture can be defined as a pattern of basic assumptions that areinvented, discovered, or developed by a given group as the organization learns to cope with the problems of external adaptation and/or internal integration (Schein, 1992). The framework is built upon two dimensions with two axes - each representing a superordinate continuum. The first dimension is the flexibility-control axis while the second dimension is the internal-external axis. The combination of these two dimensions results in four quadrants of cultural dimensions which include, namely group, developmental, hierarchical, and rational cultures.

Certain types or styles of organizational cultures have been associated with either positive or negative outcomes for organizational effectiveness or for individual employees within the organization (Schein, 1996). A study by Likert (1967), among many other studies, suggests that the type of positive, employee-focused management practices that are consistent with group culture values are likely to inspire employees to make greater efforts with their work. In the Asian work context, for example, the Korean public personnel system and practices have been significantly affected in many ways by the Confucian cultural legacies, such as collectivism, ritualism (or formalism), and hierarchical harmonization (in contrast to egalitarian harmony) (Park and Joo, 2010). Most Korean bureaucrats are inclined toward hierarchical harmony where they are presupposed to accept authority, to follow socially accepted norms of behavior, and to get along well with other members of their organizations (Baek, 1993; Cho, 1984).

1. The Concept of Organizational Culture

Schein (1992)

Culture is **a pattern of shared basic assumptions** that the group learned as it solved its problems of external adaptation and internal integration, that has worked well enough to be considered valid and, therefore, to be taught to new members as the correct way to perceive, think, and feel in relation to those problems.

Culture is the dominant pattern of living, thinking, feeling, and believing that is developed and transmitted by people, consciously or unconsciously, to subsequent generations.

Slocum & Hellriegel (2011, p. 17)

Slocum & Hellriegel (2011, p. 49)

Organizational culture reflects the shared and learned values, beliefs, and attitudes of its members. In a sense, organizational cultures is **the personality of the organization.**

Organizational cultures refers to **a system of shared meaning held by members** that distinguished the organization from other organization.

Robbins & Judge (2011, p. 554)

2. Structure of Organizational Culture

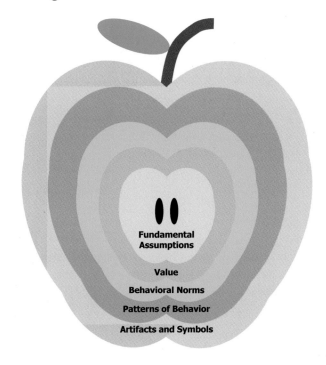

Source: Schein (1980, 1985)

3. Importance of Organizational Culture

4. Functions of Organizational Culture

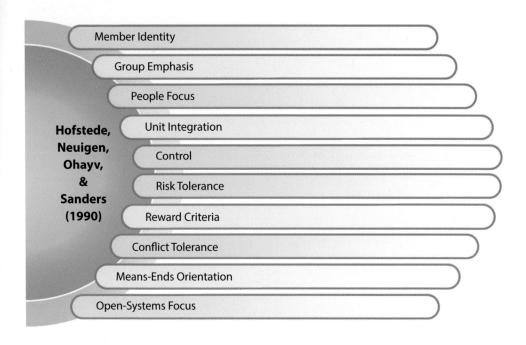

Source: Hofstede et al. (1990), Rainey (2014, pp. 356-357)

Source: Hofstede et al. (1990), Rainey (2014, pp. 356-357)

5. Type of Organizational Culture

1) Hofstede (1980)'s Point of View

① Power Distance

Power Distance

Power distance is the extent to which individuals
in a society accept status and power inequalities as a normal
and functional aspect of life.

High in Power Distance

Citizens generally accept
status and power inequalities.
Individuals who are raised in
a high power distance culture behave
submissively with leaders and
avoid disagreements with them.

Hofstede (1980)

Low in Power Distance

Citizens generally do not accept
status and power inequalities.
In Low power distance countries,
employees are expected to bypass
a leader if necessary
in order to get their work done.

Source: Slocum & Hellriegel (2011, pp. 73-74)

② Uncertainty Avoidance

Uncertainty Avoidance

Uncertainty avoidance is the extent to which individuals
rely on procedures and organizations (including government)
to avoid ambiguity, unpredictability, and risk.

High Uncertainty Avoidance

Individuals seek orderliness,
consistency, structure, formalized
procedures, and laws to
cover situations in their daily lives.
More secure long-term employment is
common in these countries.

Hofstede (1980)

Low Uncertainty Avoidance

There is strong tolerance of
ambiguity and uncertainty.
Job mobility and layoffs are
more commonly accepted in these
countries.

Source: Slocum & Hellriegel (2011, p. 74)

143

③ Individualism vs. Collectivism

Individualism vs. Collectivism
Individualism is the tendency of individuals to look after themselves and their immediate families. Collectivism is the tendency of individuals to emphasize their belonging to groups and to look after each other in exchange for loyalty.

Individualism	Hofstede (1980)	Collectivism
A culture high on individualism emphasizes individual initiative, decision making, and achievement. When group goals conflict with personal goals, individuals commonly pursue their own goals.		Groups focus on their common welfare. The sense of belonging and 'we' versus 'I' in relationships is fundamental. Group goals are generally thought to be more important than the individual's personal goals.

Source: Slocum & Hellriegel (2011, p. 73)

④ Gender Role Orientation (Masculinity vs. Femininity)

Gender Role Orientation
Gender role orientation is the extent to which a society reinforces, or does not reinforce, traditional notions of masculinity versus femininity.

Masculinity	Hofstede (1980)	Femininity
A society is called masculine when gender roles are clearly distinct. Dominant values are materials success and progress and money.		A society is called feminine when gender roles overlap. Dominant values include caring for others, emphasizing the importance of individuals, and relationships, stressing the QWL, and resolving conflict by compromise and negotiation.

Source: Slocum & Hellriegel (2011, p. 74)

144

⑤ Long-term Orientation vs. Short-term Orientation

> ### Long-Term Orientation vs. Shot-Term Orientation
>
> Long-term orientation is the extent to which the society embraces the virtues oriented toward future rewards. Shot-term orientation is seen in those societies that expect and reward quick results, view leisure time as important.

Long-Term Orientation

These countries include characteristics such as adaptation of traditions to the modern context, respect for tradition and obligation within limits, thrift, perseverance toward slow results, willingness to subordinate oneself for a purpose, and concern with virtue.

Hofstede (1980)

Short-Term Orientation

These countries have little respect for old-time traditions, and reward the risk taking and adaptability required of entrepreneurs. The main work values are freedom, individual rights, achievement, and thinking for oneself.

Source: Slocum & Hellriegel (2011, pp. 74-75)

2) Deal & Kennedy (1982)'s Point of View

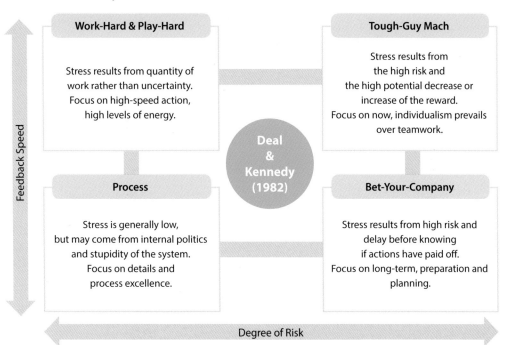

Feedback Speed

Work-Hard & Play-Hard

Stress results from quantity of work rather than uncertainty. Focus on high-speed action, high levels of energy.

Tough-Guy Mach

Stress results from the high risk and the high potential decrease or increase of the reward. Focus on now, individualism prevails over teamwork.

Deal & Kennedy (1982)

Process

Stress is generally low, but may come from internal politics and stupidity of the system. Focus on details and process excellence.

Bet-Your-Company

Stress results from high risk and delay before knowing if actions have paid off. Focus on long-term, preparation and planning.

Degree of Risk

Source: Deal & Kennedy (1982)

145

3) Quinn & Kimberly (1984)'s Point of View

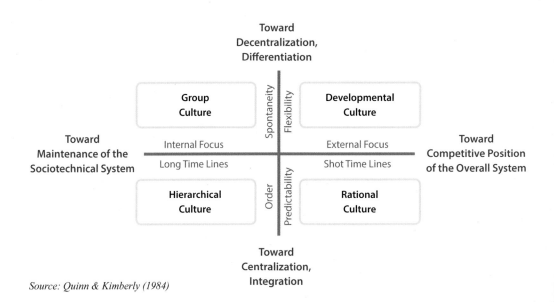

Source: Quinn & Kimberly (1984)

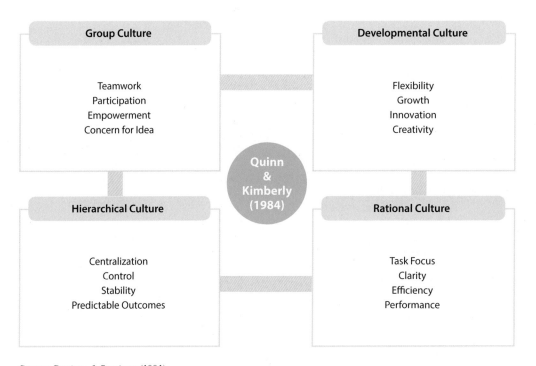

Source: Denison & Spreitzer (1991)

4) Cameron et al. (2008)'s Point of View

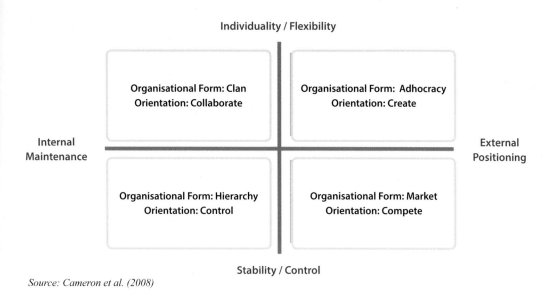

Individuality / Flexibility

Organisational Form: Clan **Orientation: Collaborate**	**Organisational Form: Adhocracy** **Orientation: Create**
Organisational Form: Hierarchy **Orientation: Control**	**Organisational Form: Market** **Orientation: Compete**

Internal
Maintenance

External
Positioning

Stability / Control

Source: Cameron et al. (2008)

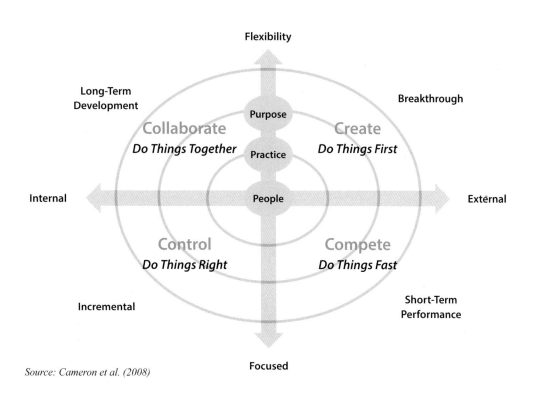

Flexibility

Long-Term
Development

Breakthrough

Collaborate
Do Things Together

Purpose

Create
Do Things First

Practice

Internal

People

External

Control
Do Things Right

Compete
Do Things Fast

Incremental

Short-Term
Performance

Focused

Source: Cameron et al. (2008)

5) Globe Studies

① Cultural Dimension

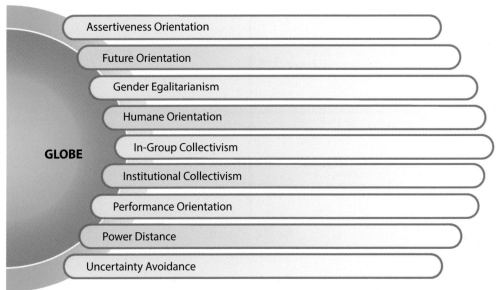

Source: House et al. (2004)

② Country Clusters According to GLOBE

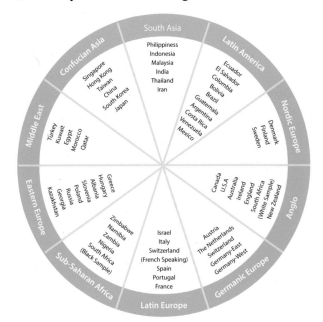

Source: House et al. (2004)

③ Cultural Clusters Classified on Cultural Dimensions

Cultural Dimension	High-Score Clusters	Low-Score Clusters
Assertiveness Orientation	Eastern Europe Germanic Europe	Nordic Europe
Future Orientation	Germanic Europe Nordic Europe	Eastern Europe Latin America Middle East
Gender Egalitarianism	Eastern Europe Nordic Europe	Middle East
Humane Orientation	Southern Asia Sub-Saharan Africa	Germanic Europe Latin Europe
In-Group Collectivism	Confucian Asia Eastern Europe Latin America Middle East Southern Asia	Anglo Germanic Europe Nordic Europe
Institutional Collectivism	Nordic Europe Confucian Asia	Germanic Europe Latin America Latin Europe
Performance Orientation	Anglo Confucian Asia Germanic Europe	Eastern Europe Latin America
Power Distance	No Clusters	Nordic Europe
Uncertainty Avoidance	Germanic Europe Nordic Europe	Eastern Europe Latin America Middle East

Source: House et al. (2004)

6. Method of Maintaining Organizational Culture

Selection   **Socialization**

Leaders

The decision maker's judgment of how well the candidates will fit into the organization, identifies people whose values are essentially consistent with at least a good portion of the organization.

The actions of top management also have a major impact on the organization's culture. Through words and behavior, senior executives establish norms that filter through the organization.

No matter how good a job the organization does in recruiting and selection, new employees are not fully indoctrinated in the organization's culture. The process that helps new employees adapt to the prevailing culture.

Source: Robbins & Judge (2011, pp. 561-564)

7. The Communication of Organizational Culture

Symbols

Physical objects, settings, and certain roles within an organization convey information about its values and basic assumptions.

Language

Slang, songs, slogans, and jargons can all carry the messages of a culture.

Organizational Culture

Narratives

The people in an organization often repeat stories, legends, sagas, and myths that convey information about the organization's history and practices.

Practices and Events

Repeated practices and special events can transmit important assumptions and values. They may include rites and ceremonies.

Source: Rainey (2014, pp. 359-360)

8. Leading Cultural Development

Make clear what leaders will monitor, ignore, measure, control

React to critical incidents and organizational crises in ways that send appropriate cultural messages

Practice deliberate role modeling, teaching, coaching

Establish effective criteria for advancement, punishment

Strategy

Coordinate organizational designs an structures with cultural messages

Design physical spaces to communicate culture

Use stories about events, people

Develop formal statements of organizational philosophy

Approach cultural leadership as comprehensive organizational change

Source: Rainey (2014, pp. 361-363)

From Theory to Practice

1. Agency Analysis

Incheon International Airport Corporation (IIAC)

Evaluating airport operations is a critical issue for all governments as well as the citizens of the world. The efficient management and safety of airports as the main door of global society is of great concern for everybody. All airports all over the world are evaluated and among them, the "World Best Airport" is selected. First time in the history of Airport Service Quality, Incheon International Airport grabbed the award for nine consecutive years (from 2005-2013).The success of IIAC can be attributed to various organizational factors that helped bring an effective and efficient airport management. For our analysis, we will dwell on the IIAC's organizational culture and its role in the successful operation of the airport.

Slocum and Hellriegel (2011) state that, "Organizational cultures are the personality of the organization." This implies the importance of organizational culture as it symbolizes the whole organization and could serve as a major source problem solving. We can take for example the China'sGuanxi network. In China, Guanxi(personal relationship) network is one of the major dynamics of Chinese society in their business dealings (Lou, 1997).Chinese applies Guanxi networks not only to business transactions but also to other circumstances wherein they share their culture, opinion, and makes many important decisions making such as buying goods, marriage, and among others. The Guanxi culture in China describes Chinese people's uniqueness in terms of dealing with each other. We can easily point reasons to understand Chinese behaviors when it comes to personal relationship or dealings. Thus, the role of organizational culture in the individual behavior is crucial. It influences decision-making and affects organizational and individual output.

Applying Quinn & Kimberly's two standards on organizational culture: (1) internal or external and (2) flexibility or stability, we analyzed IIAC's unique organizational culture. Through a survey questionnaire, majority of the respondents answered that IIAC focuses more on aspects of internal organization. This result confirmed the organization's cultural characteristic that emphasizes group and hierarchical culture. The findings on the second aspect—flexibility and stability—reveal that IIAC adapts organizational team system and confirmed a group culture of IIAC. The company is composed of more than one hundred teams embedded in various departments.

Graphical Representation of Quinn and Kimberly's Model

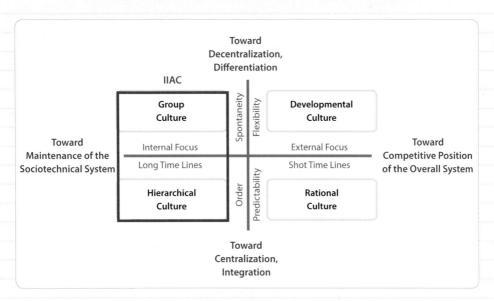

An organization that has strong group culture tends to adapt very well in a global market. Group culture is not rigid, but rather, it is flexible; it focuses more on internal relationship. It makes the organization more united, and can boost employee's loyalty in their organization. This cultural characteristic we found in IIAC provides a clear evidence of their organizational success. The global recognition as the best airport to exist in the whole world is something that requires strong commitment and dedication to service. The company and its peopleshare the same vision and are internally motivated to achieve more; and continuously promote a culture of transparency and responsibility.

Lastly, the survey reveals that IIAC employees are highly satisfied with the existing company's culture. This concludes that an employee friendly organizational culture can further motivate employees to work in order to achieve organizational vision.

Discussion Questions on Agency Case

1 For the case of IIAC, what methods and strategies could be suggested for leading cultural development? What actions can leaders take to change the organizational culture?

2 Please discuss and explain the typology of public executive entrepreneurship developed by Fellman (1986) and Marmor (1987). What are the practical implications for innovating the Korean administrative culture?

3 Prepare a memo about organizational culture in an organization with which you are familiar. Describe the dimensions of culture using any one of the models described in the chapter. Some examples include Hofstede (1980), Deal and Kennedy (1982), Quinn and Kimberly (1984), Cameron et al. (2008) and Globe Studies.

Class Exercises

1   Explain in general and then provide examples of how the following organizational characteristics affect the organization's culture:

- The design of physical spaces;
- The absence of formal statements, charters, and creeds;
- A promotion policy that gives preference to individuals with the most years of service (e.g., most of the higher positions are filled on the basis of seniority);
- The adoption of effective work-life balance/friendly policies.

2   You are the human resource director of a city department that provides various social services to the community. State regulations require that you develop hiring and retention programs that foster diversity within the workplace. Similar programs have been attempted in the past but have met with resistance. Why do you think this is the case? How would you go about gaining acceptance of your proposal?

2. Research Notes

Research Note 1

Determinants of Positive Job Attitude and Behavior
in the Asian Work Context
: Evidence from Korean Central Government Agencies

This study probes and tests the impacts of organizational commitment (OC) and organizational citizenship behaviour (OCB) among public employees in the Asian context. Using a 2010 Korean Central Government Survey of forty Korean central government agencies(totalling 1,122 respondents), an antecedent-outcome model is developed which analyses how different types of interpersonal and organizational characteristics affect OC and OCB using hierarchical and multi-level ordering statistical techniques. The research finds that certain predictors, such as trust in colleagues (TC), formalized structures, and group culture, play significant roles in fostering OC and OCB among employees. In conclusion, suggestions are made for further research, and practical implications for Asian civil servants are considered.

Research Framework

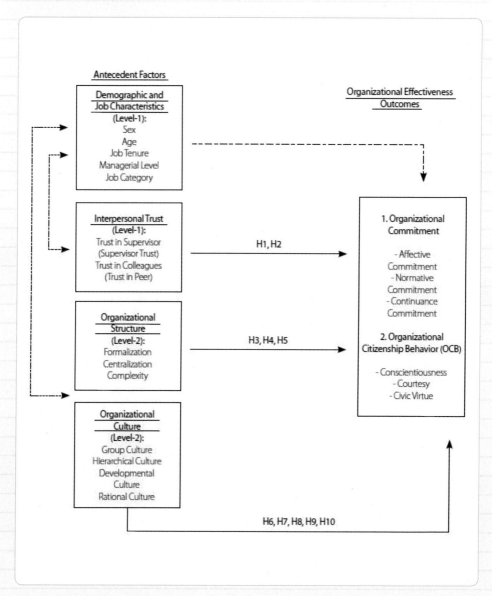

Source: Park, Park, & Ryu (2013)

The Roles of Integrative Leadership for Enhancing Organizational Effectiveness in the Chinese Public Sector

This study examines the role of Asian leadership behaviors for generating positive organizational attitudes and behaviors. The threefold purpose of this study is as follows: (1) to verify whether three leadership styles (servant, ethical, and participative) contribute to enhancing organizational trust and commitment, (2) to test the full and partial mediating roles of organizational trust and commitment in the relationship between the three leadership styles and organizational outcomes (in-role performance and managerial accountability), and (3) to probe indirect leadership impacts on performance and accountability outcomes.

Drawing on social capital and social exchange theories, we constructed a survey that measured public employees' perceptions and behaviors regarding leadership, commitment, human resource (HR) policies, perceived organizational states, OCB, job tension, and trust, using the alumni database from 2001 to 2010 of the Department of Public Administration, Zhejiang University.

We employed exploratory factor analysis (EFA) and confirmatory factor analysis (CFA) to operationalize the variables and to confirm the latent constructs from the relevant survey questions. Second, to confirm the total direct and indirect effects, we employed a full structural equation model (SEM) to test the interrelationships among variables, and to assess the relative strength of each variable. The results of this study demonstrate that ethical and participative leadership behaviors in the Chinese public sector are positively and significantly associated with organizational trust and commitment. Based on a discussion of the main findings, various research and practical implications for public management theory and practice are provided.

Research Framework

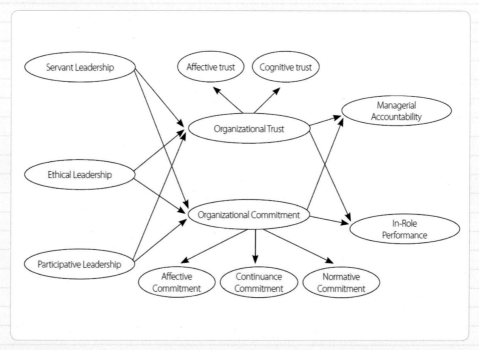

Source: Park, Miao, & Kim (2013)

Structures

Framework

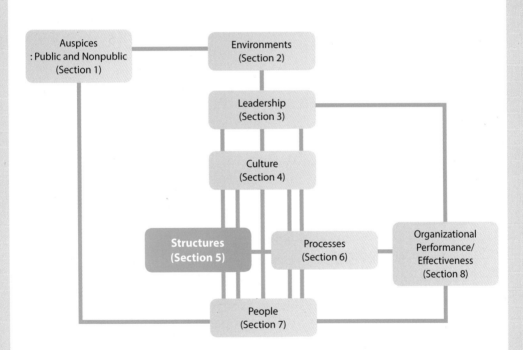

Source: Park, S. M. (2013). *Public Management: A Research Handbook*.
    Daeyoung Moonhwasa Publishing Company.

Keyword

- Organizational Structures
- Complex
- Dependence
- Not Separated
- Centralization
- Decentralization
- Complexity
- Formalization
- Red Tape
- Organizational Design

- Ideology
- Strategic Apex
- Middle Line
- Operating Core
- Techno-Structure
- Support Staff
- Professional Bureaucracy
- Adhocracy
- Machine Bureaucracy
- Simple Structure

1. Play One's Role as a Public Administrator

Design of a State Office of Energy
- Can Form Follow Function?

A large northeastern state created an Office of Energy (OE) in 1999, largely in anticipation of the energy shortages that began to emerge a few years later. But at the time of its creation, the office served only one major function: providing information concerning conservation to the public, industry, and other government agencies. The office was started on a shoestring with thirty professional and staff employees, five clerical and a budget of $1,850,000. The staff complement was only 15- nine professionals and six clerical. At the time, its simple organization structure seemed adequate. The staff included a director and assistant director that new little about energy but had experience as community organizers and publicists. The director (Corky Watt) focused most of her energy on community awareness of conservation. The assistant director (William Erg) had a more relevant background, having an MPA and a civil engineering degree, but had been chiefly deployed in developing conservation policies such as the Office's campaign to get cities to adopt long-life energy efficient bulbs for streetlights.

State Enaergy Office, circa 1999

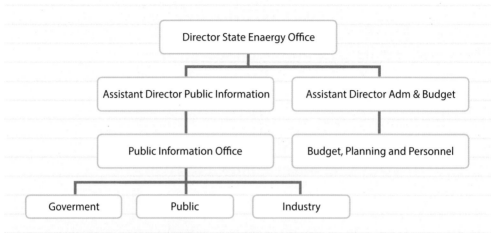

As the California natural gas calamity of 2001 occurred, along with other emergent energy problems and with environmental limitations on coal-fired power plants, the State became much more interested in its preparation for energy crises and quickly broadened and expanded the responsibilities and resources of State Energy Office. By late 2001, the number of professional and staff personnel had grown to 185 and the number of clerical and part-time personnel had grown to 45. The budget had quadrupled and then quadrupled again. The State Energy Office was not the third largest in the U.S., trailing only New York and California. In addition to its original public information program (which had itself grown considerably), the agency was now involved in a host of new, statutorily-mandated duties including:

- Setting conservation regulations,
- Small-scale sponsorship of in-state energy R&D (primarily through contracts to state universities),
- Long-range energy resource planning for the state, and
- Coordination of energy-related federal aid.

As so often happens, everyone was so caught up in the whirl of expansion that there was no time to worry about even the most basic matters pertaining to organization design. All of these new programs were integrated into the existing organization design, one devised for a "boutique" operation. Further hampering the organization, Director Corky Watt had taken another job in 2000, but before doing so, and being democratic in every way, had decided to split the Director job between the two directors, William Erg and Tatiana Volt. Volt had joined the State Energy Office in 2000 and had quickly before a favorite of Watt's due not only to her widely-attested managerial skills but her "people skills," something Erg seemed to be lacking. However, Volt's previous work was entirely in public relations, having been the media coordinator for a failed gubernatorial candidate and, before that, a public relations associate with Parker & Penn, one of the state's largest PR firms.

Despite some limitations imposed by the co-director scheme, the basic problem in late 2001, was that the now much more complex and multi-functional organization was designed on the scaffolding of the original organization. The organization design was as follows:

State Energy Office, circa 2001

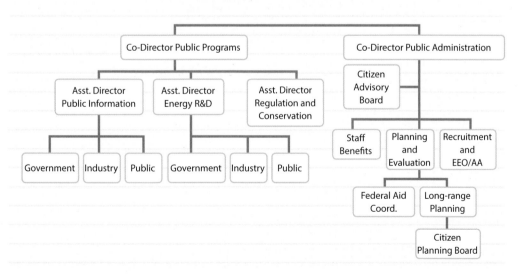

By late 2001, the organization structure became so dysfunctional that it demanded attention. After having convened a meeting of key personnel, co-directors Volt and Watt found that the most common complaints that appeared to be design and structure-related were the following:

- The most serious problem was a lack of coordination and "an inability for the right hand to know what the left hand was doing."
- Jurisdictional turf was poorly defined and functional overlap was common.
- There was no consideration of the different organizational and programmatic needs of different energy resources (e.g., solar, coal) and technologies.
- The co-directors "had too much power and not enough technical expertise."
- The citizen planning board and the citizen advisory board were getting in one another's way.
- Staff resources were being wasted with the "government," "industry," "public" organization scheme.

Source: The case was written by Dr. Hal G. Rainey

Warm-Up Questions

You are the Acme Consulting Firm, LTD. You have been hired to suggest suitable design and management changes. You are reporting to the state's Secretary of Interior, who is an elected cabinet officials to whom the State Energy Office reports. The Secretary, Iris Conangelo, has complete authority to make any changes she wishes.

You should assume that both Watt and Volt will remain, but you can put them in any managerial role you wish.

In assessing these problems:

1   Which complaints, among those listed above, do you think are most significant? Which, if any, should be given little weight?

2   How might the organization's formal structures be designed to cope with the more significant problems? How might they be designed to cope with the rapidly changing problems and policies in the field of energy?

3   Most important, provide a design. Make sure you provide a rationale for everything you suggest. Make sure you have a schematic (e.g., organizational chart) that reflects you suggestions. You need not limit your work, however, to concepts easily conveyed in an organization chart.

Source: The discussion questions were based on the case written by Dr. Hal G. Rainey

2. Play One's Role as a Government Reformer

Let's suppose you are the manager of Organization Management Strategy Office (OMSO) under the Ministry of Public Management in Korea. The Minister sent a memorandum via email directing your office to undertake an organizational structural change applicable for the Korea public organization. Please read the memorandum for the whole details of the directives and let's try to comply with the order of the Minister.

From Minister Sup-Jong Cho (minsiter_mpm@korea.com) You moved this message to its current location.

Sent Monday, May 22, 20153:34:29 PM

To OM Strategy Office (omso_mpm@korea.com)

2 attachment | Download all as zip (1234.0 KB) Structures Reform Plan.docx (698.0 KB) Emphasis on Hierarchy Hampers Globalization. docx (536.0 KB)

View online

MEMORANDUM-MPM0003

TO: The Manager, Organization Management Strategy Office (OMSO)
RE: Submission of Public Organizational Structure Reform Plan
FROM: The Minister, Ministry of Public Management
DATE: 22 December 2014

- -

The Korea public organization has its unique foundational origin that nurtured a distinct organizational culture, structure, and processes. Some considered these characteristics as strength; however, others argue that they are no longer applicable in the contemporary public management strategies, thus necessitate reform. Local and foreign public administration practitioners and scholars share the same notion for the need of an organizational structural review.

In this regard, I hereby direct your office to carefully study the possibility of undertaking a comprehensive structural reform for our public organization. Concomitantly, draft and submit the results of your study that will serve as our government's blueprint that will detail the general and specific structural reform for our government. We will submit the same to the Office of the President for her perusal and consideration. I would like you to give a serious attention and provide an elaborate response on the following issues:

a. What are the main informal and formal structural characteristics of public agencies in Korea (e.g., organizational size, subunit size, span of control, organizational level, hierarchical shape, and administrative intensity, etc.)?

b. What do you think are the negative impacts on organizational effectiveness that may arise from such characteristics?

c. Please discuss how to resolve these issues.

We must be aware that there is urgency for this endeavor. Personally, I see this effort as critical in boosting our nation's competitiveness in the era of globalization.

For your immediate action and compliance.

Attached File 1: Problem-Based Learning (PBL)

Structure Reform Plan

	Step	Contents		
1	Environments/ Conditions/ Backgrounds	Please explain the situation briefly.		
2	Problem Definition	In your own perspective, please be as specific as possible when pointing out the problem.		
3	Actual Case Studies	Please explain by giving specific examples (Newspaper articles, news clips, or Interviews)		
4	Finding Alternatives	Possible Solutions	Merits/Pros in a Korean Context	Demerits/Cons in a Korean Context
		①		
		②		
		③		
5	The Best Solution	Why did you choose this alternative as the best solution? What are the expected effects and potential contribution?		

Attached File 2

Emphasis on Hierarchy Hampers Globalization

Corporate Sector Needs to Rethink 'Punishment Culture'

to Make Officials Willing to Take Risks

... It was an appropriate allocation of responsibility, given the strong Confucian discipline of national governance at the time. But it did lead to some problems in 'interfacing' with the Western world, since the strict protocol requirements concentrated more on issues of who was allowed to communicate with whom, depending on status and rank, rather than on the substance of the proposals being made. ...

... It is one of the major sources of confusion and misunderstanding between Koreans and Westerners that the hierarchy of relationships is so very important in this country. If I describe someone, for example, as a "friend," and that person happens to be a decade or so younger than me, my Korean counterpart may ask "How can someone so much younger be your friend?"

Also, it can be amusing for a foreigner to watch how the courtesy of yielding the "president's seat" at the right-hand rear of the car is acted out when businessmen share a ride. In the west, the best seat is, if not the driver's seat behind the wheel, then probably the front seat next to the driver, on the grounds that it provides the best views of the passing scenery. ...

... Second, Korean corporate life, which is run with the same discipline as a military organization, placing the same emphasis on hierarchy, status and the following of orders, may be becoming steadily obsolete as a business culture, out of tune with the environment where many Korean firms have to operate as they invest in overseas operations. ...

A society that is run exclusively by those at the top of the age ladder is likely to be more resistant to change, slower to generate new ideas, less flexible and less well equipped to survive in today's rapidly shifting commercial, political and social milieus. In an era of competition between countries and societies, Korea needs to equip itself with the tools of success and survival, not ageism.

Source: The information contained in this article was extracted from
"The Korea Times (2008.11.24)" by Alan Timblick

2 Theory Synopsis

Section 5 explores the nature of organizational culture in relation to dominant Western models and analyzes its most crucial features. In addition, drawing on a set of actual cases, this section provides an opportunity to probe whether hierarchical, centralized, and formalized structures associated with Confucian societies are able to nurture positive job attitudes and behaviors of public employees, as differently anticipated in Western contexts. For example, previous studies found that hierarchical, centralized, and formalized structures have significant and typically negative effects on positive job attitudes and behaviors (see, for example, George & Jones, 1997; Lawrence & Lorsch, 1967).

From an agency theory perspective, the critical issue of public management seems to be the extent to which an organization requires strict control and close monitoring of employees. According to the principal-agent theory, the actions of managers – acting in the role of principals – are usually dictated by organizational factors such as structure, policies, and culture; and managers are expected to exert these concerns over the actions of their employees. Many public management researchers have investigated whether government bureaucracies have distinctive and peculiar structural and legal characteristics, as well as how and to what extent these characteristics impact organizational performance (Downs, 1967; Brewer & Walker, 2013). While an overall, single measure of organizational structure has not been established, the use of discrete dimensions of organizational structures to evaluate performance includes features of formalization, centralization, and complexity.

1. The Concept of Organizational Structure

1) Organizational Structure Definition

Rainey (2014, p. 211)

Management researchers use the term structure to refer to the configuration of the hierarchical levels and specialized units and positions within an organization and to the formal rules governing these arrangements.

The way in which job tasks are formally divided, grouped, and coordinated.

Robbins & Judge (2011)

Mintzberg (1979)

The sum total of the ways in which it divides its labor into distinct tasks and then achieves coordination among them.

2) Structural Characteristics of Public Organizations

Downs (1967)

Downs (1967) argues that government bureaucracies inevitably move toward rigidity and hierarchical constraints. Government bureaucracies have exceedingly complex rules, red tape, and hierarchies, even in comparison with large private organizations.

Many organization theorists regard other factors – such as organizational size, environmental complexity, and technology – as more important influences on structure than public or private status.

Rainey (2014)

Source: Downs (1967), Rainey (2014, p. 212)

Pugh et al. (1969)

Authority more concentrated at the top in public organizations; no difference in structuring of activities.

Little difference in employees' perceptions regarding levels of formalization about their jobs and communications.

Kurland & Egan (1999)

175

Complex   Dependence

Not Separated

Macrostructure of
public organizations
is complex.

Structure within public
organizations is not easily
separated form structure
outside.
Internal structures
are attributes of our
government.

Major institutional
attributes may differ
depending on such
factors as constitutional
requirements.

Source: Rainey (2014, p. 240)

2. Measures of Organizational Structure

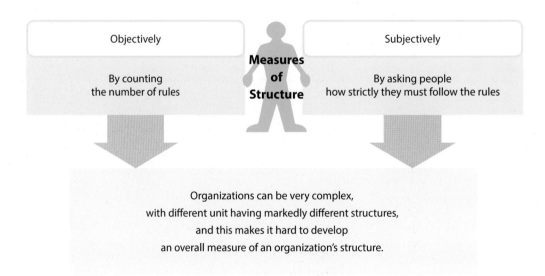

Objectively	Measures of Structure	Subjectively
By counting the number of rules		By asking people how strictly they must follow the rules

Organizations can be very complex,
with different unit having markedly different structures,
and this makes it hard to develop
an overall measure of an organization's structure.

Source: Rainey (2014, p. 216)

3. Dimensions of Organizational Structure

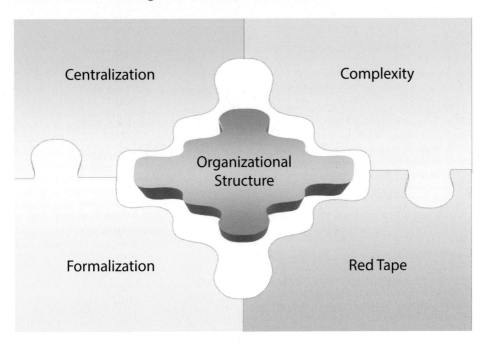

1) Centralization

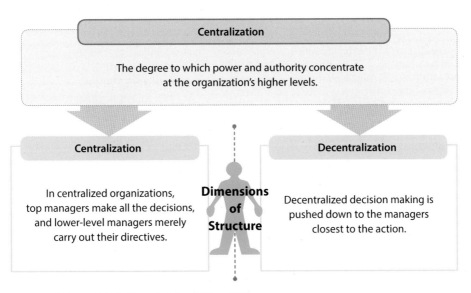

Source: Rainey (2014, p. 216), Robbins & Judge (2011, p. 527)

2) Complexity

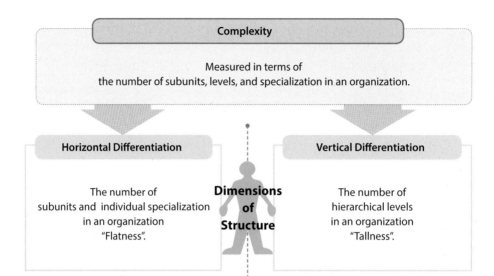

Source: Rainey (2014, p. 217)

3) Formalization

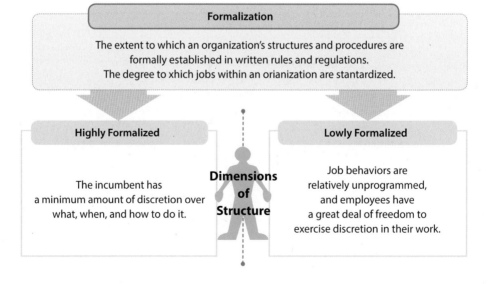

Source: Rainey (2014, pp. 216-217), Robbins & Judge (2011, pp. 527-528)

4) Red Tape

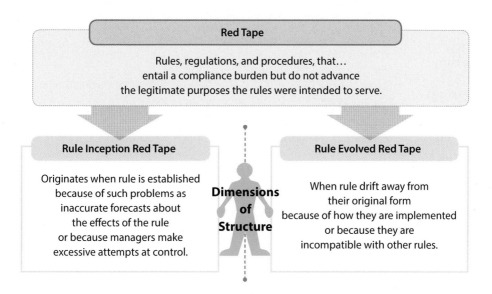

Source: Rainey (2014, p. 217)

4. Influences on Structure

Source: Rainey (2014, pp. 217-223)

179

5. The Meaning of the Organizational Design

Slocum & Hellriegel (2011, p. 448)

The process of selecting a structure for the tasks, responsibilities, and authority relationships within an organization.

An organization's design influences communication patterns among individuals and teams and determines which person or department has the political power to get things done.

Slocum & Hellriegel (2011, p. 448)

6. Galbraith's Organizational Design Strategies

Organizations face varying degrees of uncertainty, depending on how much more information they need than they actually have.

As this uncertainty increases, the organizational structure must process more information.

Galbraith (1997) proposed a set of techniques for designing and coordinating activities based on information processing.
He defines uncertainty as the gap between the information that is required and the information that is possessed by the organization.

Rainey (2014)

Source: Galbraith (1997), Rainey (2014, p. 224)

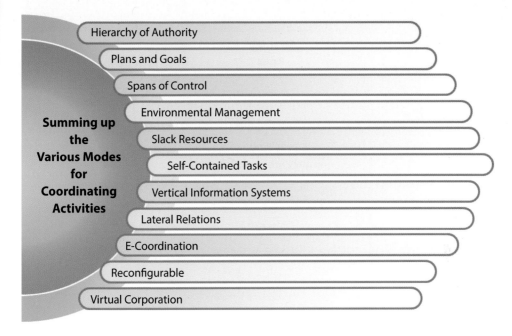

Source: Galbraith (2002), Rainey (2014, p. 224)

7. Mintzberg's Synthesis

1) Six Components of Organizations

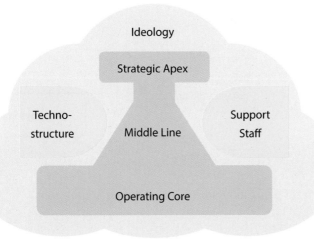

Source: Mintzberg (1979)

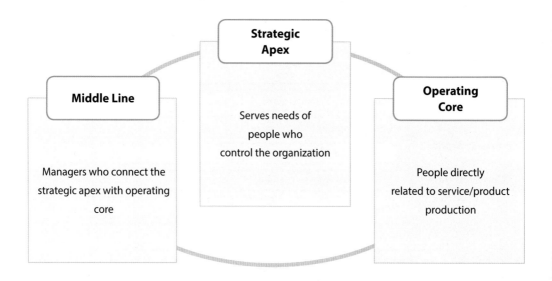

Source: Mintzberg (1979)

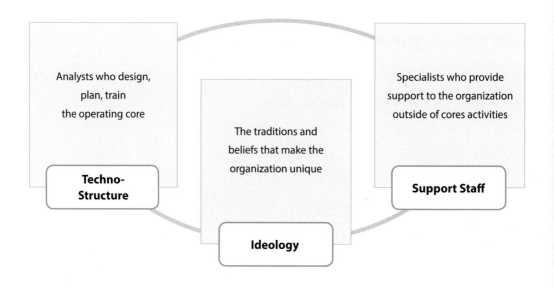

Source: Mintzberg (1979)

2) Design Parameters

Design of Positions

Individual Positions can be
established through
job specialization, behavior formalization,
and training and indoctrination.

Design of Superstructures

All organizations do this in part
through unit grouping,
based on any of a number of criteria
: Knowledge and skill, function, time, output,
clients, or place.

Organizational Design

Design of Lateral Linkages

Organizations can use
performance-control systems,
Action-planning systems, or liaison devices.

Design of Decision-Making Systems

Vertical decentralization involves pushing
decision-making authority down to lower
levels. Horizontal decentralization involves
spreading authority out to staff analysts or
experts or across individuals
involved in the work or the organization.

Source: Mintzberg (1979), Rainey (2014, pp. 225-228)

3) Types of Organizational Structures

Environmental Complexity (Complex → Simple)

Professional Bureaucracy

Complex & Stable
Decentralized; Bureaucratic;
Standardized Skills

Adhocracy

Complex & Dynamic
Decentralized; Organic;
Mutual Adjustment

Type of Organizational Structures

Machine Bureaucracy

Simple & Stable
Centralized; Bureaucratic;
Standardized Work Processes;
Direct Supervision from Strong Strategic
Apex

Simple Structure

Simple & Dynamic
Centralized; Organic;
Direct Supervision

Environmental Stability (Stable → Dynamic)

Source: Mintzberg (1979)

4) Major Design Alternatives

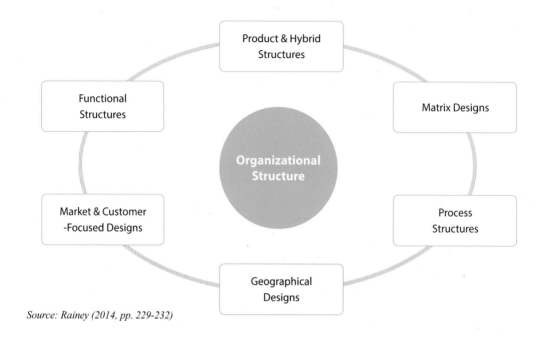

Source: Rainey (2014, pp. 229-232)

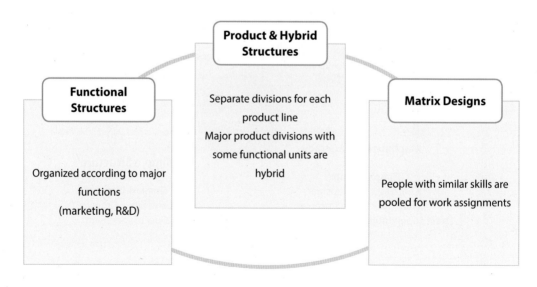

Source: Rainey (2014, pp. 229-232)

Functional Structure

```
                              CEO
```

Vice President, Operation	Vice President, Marketing	Vice President, Finance	Vice President, HR	Vice President, R&D
Plant Managers	Regional Sales Managers	Controller	Labor Relations Director	Scientific Director
Shift Supervisors	District Sales Managers	Accounting Supervisor	Plant HR Managers	Lab Manager

Product and Hybrid Structure

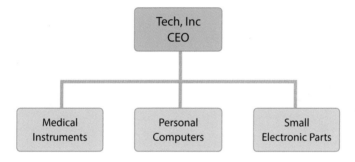

```
                        Tech, Inc
                          CEO
```

Medical Instruments	Personal Computers	Small Electronic Parts

Matrix Design

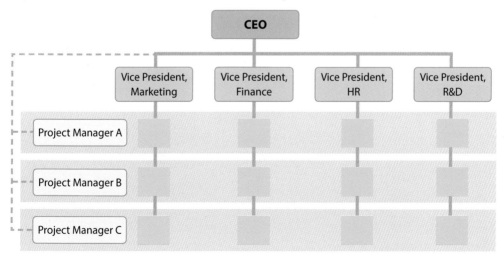

```
                              CEO
```

	Vice President, Marketing	Vice President, Finance	Vice President, HR	Vice President, R&D
Project Manager A				
Project Manager B				
Project Manager C				

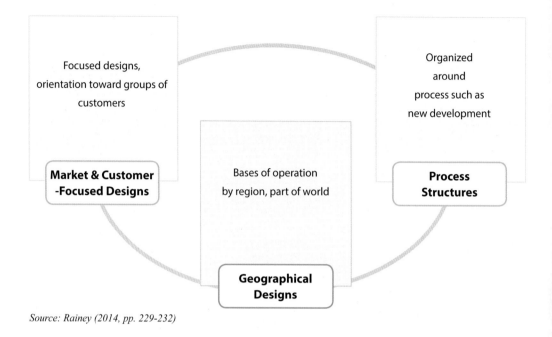

Source: Rainey (2014, pp. 229-232)

8. Determinants and Outcomes of Organizational Structure

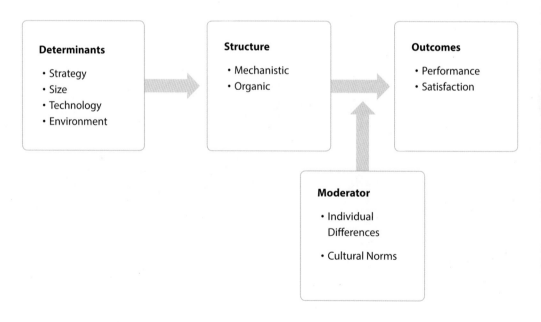

Source: Robbins & Judge (2011, p. 545)

From Theory to Practice

1. Agency Analysis

The Board of Audit and Inspection of Korea

The Board of Audit and Inspection (BAI) is a constitutional agency and the central audit agency of the Republic of Korea. The Korean Constitution, in Article 97 provides the general duties and responsibilities of the BAI.

Article 97 [Board of Audit and Inspection] of the South Korea Constitution provides that:

> *"The Board of Audit and Inspection is established under the direct jurisdiction of the President to inspect and examine the settlement of the revenues and expenditures of the State, the accounts of the State, and other organizations specified by law and the job performances of the executive agencies and public officials."*

The fundamental law of the land defines the agency's functions and mandates to promote transparency in all governmental transactions. Specifically, BAI must conduct auditing and inspection of all government revenues and expenditures, in all government levels and its subsidiaries. Although BAI is under the auspices of the President, he cannot interfere on the duties and functions of the agency. BAI maintains independence and must dispose its mandate without fear of political influences.

Despite the constitutionally guaranteed independence, it seems that the BAI is still under the skirts of influence of the President. The chairman of the agency is chosen and appointed by the President. The political parties, both administration party and the opposition, kept arguing on the appointments done by the President. Due to political bickering, there are times that the position of chairman was vacant for a period of time. The extent of external influence on the agency is very strong compared to other public organizations. Thus, the analysis will be anchored on the identification of different factors that influence BAI and determine the distinct BAI's organizational components such as structure, culture, environment, and its people. Particularly, this analysis will give emphasis on the organizational structure drawing on its four dimensions: (1) degree of centralization, (2) formalization, (3) red tape, and (4) complexity.

Four Dimensions of Organizational Structure

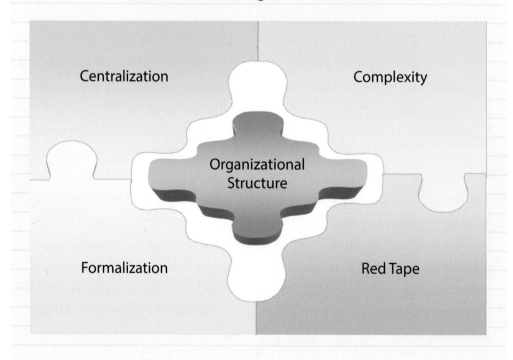

1) Organizational Structure of BAI: Four Dimensional Analyses

□ Degree of Centralization

BAI system is generally not that centralized. Of course, BAI's top management is powerfulbecause they make important decisions, but lower-level managers also can make decisions and carry out agency's plans. Unlike with the common perception of centralized decision-making, BAI's leadership in different levels like middle-level managers have appropriate authorities and decision-making powers; they make decisions freely and even propose policy ideas to the top management level.

□ Formalization

Formalization is the extent in which organization's structure and procedures are formally established in written rules and regulation. By this concept, we can assume BAI as a highly formalized organization that follows strict standard operating procedures. Highly formalized organization is often criticized because of its rigidity but it enables stable operation of organization. For example, the absence or vacancy in the agency's top leadership cannot derail the functioning of the office. A policy in place encourages automatic assumption of next top leader in rank to assume the leadership of the agency until an official appointment is approved for the chairman.

□ Red Tape

Red tape describes the bureaucratic nature of public organization's processes that must adhere to certain rules and formalities. The basic notion on government red tape is being oppressively complex—one must follow the specified procedures— and heavily time consuming. In the BAI, the nature of their work requires a careful documentation and strict compliance of requirements provided by law. For example, inspection and reporting of alleged misappropriation of government funds are serious allegations that must skillfully comply with the letters of the law and agency policies. There are no shortcuts; everything must be in accordance with the law. For the BAI, red tape is of no issue. Inevitably, their office must comply with the standards provided for reporting, investigation, and inspection of various government agency's revenues and expenditures.

□ Complexity

Like other public sectors, BAI's complexity entails both horizontal and vertical differentiation. BAI displays some hierarchical characteristics but it's not that high. Instead, its complexity structure focuses more on horizontal differentiation. The organizational structure of BAI shows a typical but flexible formation. The upper echelon—the chairman and the council of commissioners—and below it are the functional departments that specifically attend to government agencies and subsidiaries. The name of the office or division will always go in tandem with the existing government agencies. If it changes name, BAI's unit that focuses on it will follow through. For example, the Ministry of Public Administration and Security (MOPAS) was changed to the Ministry of Security and Public Administration (MOSPA), thus BAI changed its department to audit department of MOSPA as well.

2) Mintzberg's Synthesis

Applying the Mintzberg's classification of organizational structure (i.e., professional bureaucracy, adhocracy, machine bureaucracy, and simple structure), we are going to widen our understanding of the BAI's prevailing organizational structure.

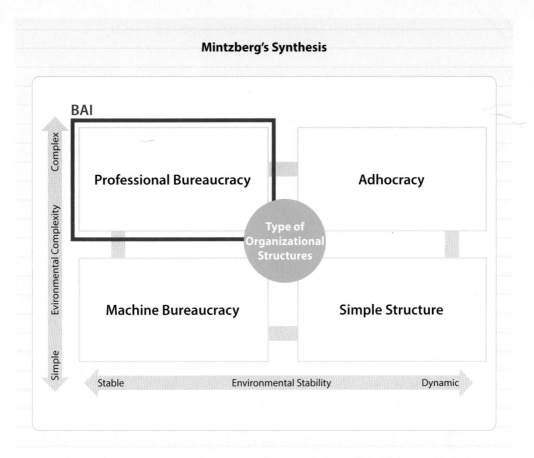

Mintzberg's Synthesis

Undoubtedly, BAI is a professional bureaucracy that adheres to government professionalism in terms of its personnel recruitment and work ethics. The agency follows a top-down decision-making approach; however, each lower level manager has an independent decision-making power and authority. Like other public sectors, BAI follows bureaucratic practices such as observation of regulation, procedure, formalized and standardized skills. Bureaucracy is necessarily stiff but environmentally stable. Unlike in a machine bureaucracy, BAI's core functions are led mostly of specialists and experts of inspection and investigation. Government audit, for example, requires a skillful or experts to do the works—sensitive and involves technical and legal issues.

Discussion Questions on Agency Case

1   What are the design strategies that Galbraith describes? What are the design
    parameters that Mintzberg describes, and what are the types of organizations
    in his typology? How do you explain the structures of BAI from both of the
    aforementioned perspectives?

2   What major design alternatives that were proposed by Galbraith could be
    applicable to the BAI case?

Class Exercises

1   What do we know about structural differences/similarities between public
    and private organizations? How do different levels of uncertainty affect the
    organizational structure? How does IT influence organization design? Please
    share your opinions about these matters drawing upon the BAI case.

2. Research Notes

Research Note 1

Working Across the Divide
: Job Involvement in the Public and Nonprofit Sectors

Job involvement is a principal factor in the lives of most people; employees in the workplace are mentally and emotionally influenced by their degree of involvement in work. Using the data from the National Administrative Studies Project III, this study empirically compares the level of job involvement between managers in the public and nonprofit sectors and explores different aspects including demographic, managerial, and institutional factors that contribute to the apparent differences. The results of the study indicate that the mean level of nonprofit managers' job involvement is significantly greater than for public managers. Each sector had specific variables that significantly and uniquely contributed to job involvement. Overall, the results suggest a need to more fully investigate the various mechanisms and functions of situational and organizational contexts, organizational norms, and culture that were associated with job involvement regardless of sector. Implications and limitations of this research are also discussed.

Research Framework

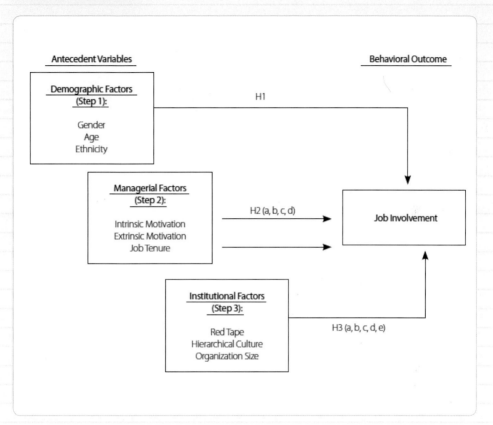

Source: Word & Park (2009)

Research on Accountability
in the Korean Central Government Agencies
: Exploring Antecedent and Moderating Effects of
Public Service Motivation, Goal Clarity,
and Person-Organization Fit

Using hierarchical regression analysis, this study tests hypotheses about the antecedent and moderating effects of three dimensions of public service motivation (PSM) (rational, normative, and affective motivation) and two types of goal orientation (goal clarity and goal congruence, i.e., personal–organization [P-O] fit) on two different work dispositions (internal accountability and external accountability) among central government officials employed in Korean public agencies. The results show that goal clarity and goal congruence substantially explain the variations of accountability of Korean public employees. Affective PSM is especially important to the outcomes. Analysis of cross-interaction effects among PSM dimensions, goal clarity, and goal congruence on outcome variables support self-perception theory's prediction that when individuals are more exposed to unstable and ambiguous organizational environments, the relationship between PSM (especially affective and normative) and accountability becomes more pronounced. Theoretical and practical implications and limitations of this research are also discussed.

Research Framework

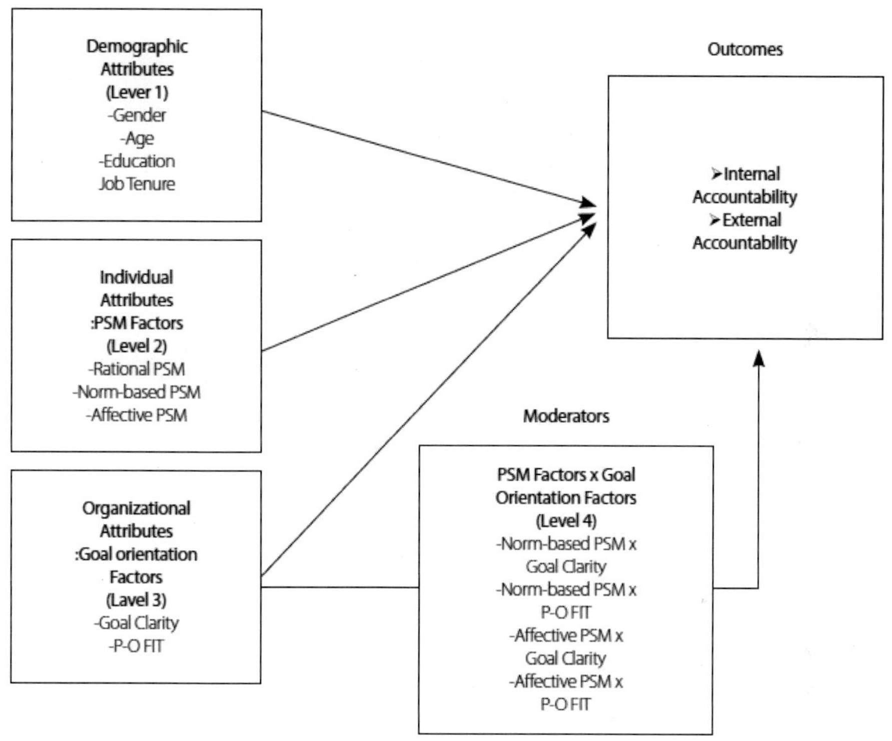

Source: Park & Kim (2013)

Processes

Framework

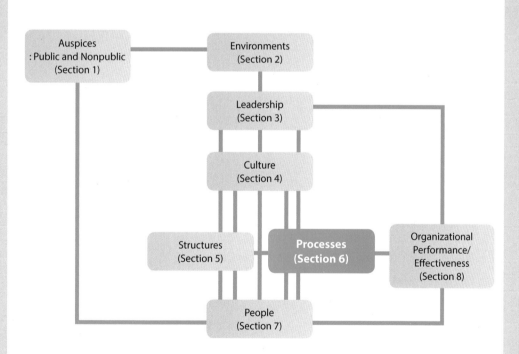

Source: Park, S. M. (2013). *Public Management: A Research Handbook*.
Daeyoung Moonhwasa Publishing Company.

Keyword

- Power Relationships
- Empowerment
- Decision Making
- Certainty
- Uncertainty
- Risk
- Communication
- Downward Communication
- Upward Communication
- Lateral Communication
- Conflict
- Intrapersonal Conflict
- Interpersonal Conflict
- Intragroup Conflict
- Intergroup Conflict
- Avoiding
- Accommodating
- Compromising
- Forcing
- Collaborating

1 Role Play Simulation

1. Play One's Role as a Public Administrator

Identifying the Dimensions

The organizational chart of the Indiana Professional Licensing Agency (PLA) is illustrated below. Its mission, as stated on the agency's website, is "To provide efficient and effective administrative support services to Indiana's professional licensing boards and commissions in order to facilitate the delivery of competent consumer services by regulated professionals to the citizens of Indiana . . . and further to provide an expedient licensing process for regulated professionals by maintaining a climate that fosters the growth of commerce while ensuring the health, safety and welfare of the citizens of our great state."

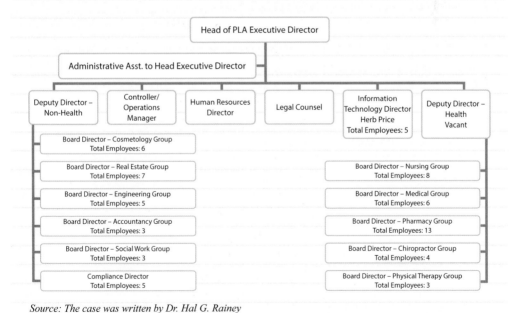

Source: The case was written by Dr. Hal G. Rainey.

Warm-Up Questions

We have discussed organizational structure, design, technology, and information technology. This exercise provides an opportunity to consider the organizational structure of a public agency in detail and to discuss its implications.

Discuss the following questions as a group and prepare brief responses/ comments to present to the class (When dividing questions among groups, questions 3, 4, 7, 8, and 9 are likely to require the most time).

1   Who does the PLA serve? Who does the PLA's main clientele serve? Is this evident in the organizational chart?

2   What structural types can be identified within the chart (functional, product/ service, hybrid, matrix, market/customer, etc.)?

3   Are there clear chains of command? Where?

4   What environmental stimuli might you expect in this type of organization? How could the structure be adjusted to rapidly respond to changes in regulations that guide the agency or its main clients?

5   What are the benefits of the design characteristics? What are the disadvantages?

6   Do you think the structure of the organization is consistent with its mission? Is the mission or part of the mission reflected in the chart? What structural reforms, if any, would you suggest to align the organizational structure with its mission?

7 How could the structure be adjusted to reflect a regional focus?

8 Using the chapter on organizational goals and effectiveness as a guide, do you see any problems with the organization's goals (as stated)? How could the structure be adjusted so client group possesses its own expertise in the areas of accounting or other major functions?

9 If the PLA decided to monitor consumer complaints for each group, how might its structure be adjusted? What structural changes would you suggest for direct monitoring of complaints? What structural changes would you suggest for indirect monitoring of complaints? What resistance to these types of reforms could you expect? How would you address the resistance?

10 Can you identify interdependencies in the organization chart? Use the chart and the types and definitions of interdependencies to explain alternatives for processing complaints.

Source: The discussion questions were based on the case written by Dr. Hal G. Rainey

2. Play One's Role as a Government Reformer

Let's suppose you are the CEO of the Government Conflict Management Strategy (GCMS), a consultancy firm based in Seoul, Korea. Your company has been engaged to various government projects that address organizational issues such as HRM, organizational development (OD), performance management, change management, and public organizational processes. Recognizing your firm's active and successful collaboration with the central and local government agencies both domestic and abroad, the Minister of the Ministry of Public Management sent you an email engaging your company's services in the development of Korea's Public Organizational Process Reform Strategy. Please read the email below and try to determine strategic approaches to satisfy the Minister's service request.

From Minister Sup-Jong Cho (minsiter_mpm@korea.com) You moved this message to its current location.

Sent Thursday, May 21, 2014 3:34:29 PM

To Seona Kim (gcmschairman@gcms.com)

3 attachment | Download all as zip (1802.0 KB) Intention Letter.docx (568.0 KB) Request for Processes Reform Plan_mpm.docx (698.0 KB) The Creativity Gap .docx (536.0 KB)

View online

Seona Kim, Ph.D.
Chief Executive Officer (CEO)
GCMS, Korea

Dear Dr. Kim,

We are astonished with the extent and success of your company's consultancy services rendered globally as well as to our local and central agencies. Indeed, it's worth engaging with your company. The regular column of your company in the broadsheet, Seoul Times, dealing with the peculiar problems of public organizational processes are worth reading and are useful materials for practitioners, scholars, and students of public management.

In your Seoul Times column dated May 12, 2014, you explicitly discussed the nuts and bolts of communication gap between the managers and subordinate employees. You correctly pointed out that such issue is unfortunate because it derails effective communication and may give rise to other problem such as conflict between leaders and followers; thus, brings flaws to organizational process.

The problems you specified in your article clearly depict prevailing issues in the public organizational process here in Korea. The strategies you revealed are enlightening, but I am a bit wary if these are applicable to our context. Thus, we decided to invite your company to work with us in the determination of possible strategic measures to address the worsening lapses in our public organizational processes.

Attached herewith is the proposed terms of engagement specifying among others the target output of the service contract:

A. Assessment of Korea's Public Organizational Process
 - In this project, we wish the following issues must be addressed:
  a. What are the main characteristics of Korea's private and public organizational processes?
  b. What are the unique characteristics of public organizational structures?
  c. What do you think are the possible problems that may arise from such characteristics? And, what are the possible measures to address those problems?

B. Korea Public Organizational Process Strategic Reform Plan

Thank you very much and hope to hear from you soon.

Truly yours,

Sup-Jong Cho
Minister,
Ministry of Public Management

Attached File 1: Problem-Based Learning (PBL)

Request for Processes Reform Plan

	Step	Contents		
1	Environments/ Conditions/ Backgrounds	Please explain the situation briefly.		
2	Problem Definition	In your own perspective, please be as specific as possible when pointing out the problem.		
3	Actual Case Studies	Please explain by giving specific examples (Newspaper articles, news clips, or Interviews)		
4	Finding Alternatives	Possible Solutions	Merits/Pros in a Korean Context	Demerits/Cons in a Korean Context
		①		
		②		
		③		
5	The Best Solution	Why did you choose this alternative as the best solution? What are the expected effects and potential contribution?		

Attached File 2

The Creativity Gap

John Burton

It might appear that Korea is already half way to becoming the "creative economy" that President Park Geun-hye wants to achieve during her administration. ...

... But one thing still threatens to kill that dream: Korea's top-down management approach that often stifles creativity. Government ministries and big companies are still run like the military, with loyalty and hierarchy, not ideas, being the highest-prized values. Changing that mindset will be exceedingly difficult.

The roots of Korea's preference for centralization lie deep. They reflect the strong influence that neo-Confucianism has had on Korea over the last 600 years after it was adopted as the guiding philosophy of the Joseon Kingdom. Korea's first exposure to modern administrative practices occurred during the Japanese colonial period and Park Chung-hee's authoritarian rule reinforced the militaristic tendencies of government and business administration.

These conditions are not ones that allow innovative businesses to thrive, although Koreans display a strong streak of entrepreneurship when the environment is right. They have the highest percentage of small business ownership among all ethnic groups in the U.S. ...

Source: The information contained in this article was extracted from
"The Korea Times (2013.06.05)" by **John Burton**

Theory Synopsis

Organizational researchers have paid attention to the importance of organizational social processes, with emphasis on the direct, indirect, or mediating roles of communication and exchange processes among organizational constituents. These processes include social communications and coordination of information and ideas, collaborative and networked relationships, and the creation and transfer of knowledge (Kogut & Zander, 1996). Especially, the whole entity of the structures and processes of social and organizational communication can also be conceptualized by the theoretical perspectives of social capital. Social capital refers to any type of social structure that creates, develops, and facilitates individual actions and decisions, and hence generates autonomous motivational behaviors within that social structure (Coleman, 1990; Crossan, Lane, White & Djurfeldt, 1995; Seibert, Kraminer, & Liden, 2001). Organizational social capital increases when organizational constituents communicate in a way that facilitates access to social resources (Coleman, 1990). Section 6 broadly examines issues related to organizational processes and communications, with a focus on power relationships, decision making processes, communications, and organizational conflicts. In addition, through case analyses and exercises, we expect that readers could recognize the barriers to effective communications and acknowledge effective ways to encourage supportive communications and to improve communication in the public sector.

1. Power Relationships

1) A Definition of Power

Robbins & Judge (2011, p. 454)

Power refers to a **capacity** that A has to **influence** the behavior of B so B acts in accordance with A's wishes.

The most important aspect of power is that it is a function of **dependency**. The greater B's dependence on A, the greater A's power in the relationships.

Robbins & Judge (2011, p. 454)

2) Source of Power

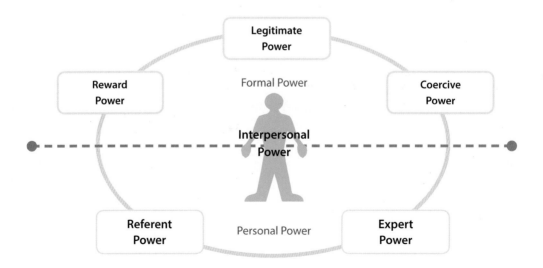

Source: Slocum & Hellriegel (2011, pp. 292-295)

① Formal Power

Legitimate Power

Power is an individual's ability to influence other's behaviors because of the person's formal position in the organization.

Reward Power

Power is an individual's ability to influence others' behaviors by providing them with valued things (praise, promotion, money, time off, and so on).

Coercive Power

Power is an individual's ability to other's behaviors by punishing them. The coercive power base depends on fear of the negative results from failing to comply.

Source: Slocum & Hellriegel (2011, pp. 292-295)

② Personal Power

Personal Power

Power is an individual's ability to influence others because they respect, admire, or like the person.
Referent power is based on identification with a person who has desirable resources or personal traits.

Power is an individual's ability to influence others' behavior because of recognized competencies, talents, or specialized knowledge.

Referent Power

Expert Power

Source: Slocum & Hellriegel (2011, pp. 292-295)

3) Power Tactics

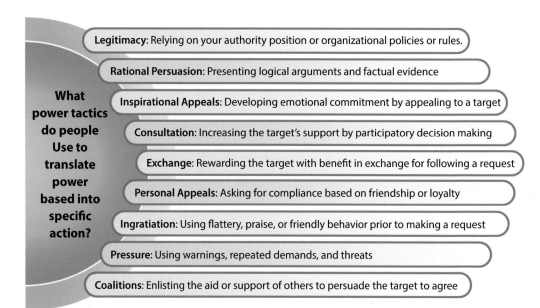

Source: Robbins & Judge (2011, pp. 459-460)

4) Empowerment

Petter et al. (2002)

Empowerment is multidimensional. It can involved such provisions as involvement in agency decisions, skill development, job autonomy, and encouragement creativity and initiative.

Empowerment means giving employees the authority, skills, and self-control to perform their tasks.

Slocum & Hellriegel (2011, p.151)

2. Decision Making

1) A Definition of Decision Making

Slocum & Hellriegel (2011, p. 416)

Decision Making includes defining problems, gathering information, generating alternatives, and choosing a course of action.

Decisions are affected by many factors. In addition to identifying and measuring the strength of these factors, leaders must estimate their potential impact.

Slocum & Hellriegel (2011, p. 417)

2) Decision Making Conditions

Certainty		Uncertainty
Certainty is the condition under which individuals are fully informed about a problem, alternative solutions are known, and the results of each solution are known	**Decision Making**	Uncertainty is the condition under which an individual does not have the necessary information to assign probabilities to the outcomes of alternative solutions

Risk

Risk refer to the condition under which individuals can define a problem, specify the probability of certain events, identify alternative solutions, and state the probability of each solution leading to a result

Source: Slocum & Hellriegel (2011, pp. 417-420)

3. Communication

1) A Definition of Communication

Robbins & Judge (2011, p. 376)

Communication must include both the **transfer** and the **understanding of meaning.**

Interpersonal communication refers to a limited number of people who are usually in proximity to each other, use many sensory channels, and are able to provide immediate feedback.

Slocum & Hellriegel (2011, p. 256)

2) Functions of Communication

Control

When employees are required to communicate any job-related grievance to their immediate boss,
To follow their job description, or to comply with company policies, communication is performing a control function.

Motivation

Communication fosters motivation by clarifying to employee what they must do, how well they are doing, and how to improve performance if it's subpar.

Communication

Emotional Expression

The communication within the group is a fundamental mechanism by with members show their satisfaction and frustrations.
Communication provides for the emotional expression of feelings and fulfillment of social needs.

Information

Communication is promoting decision making.
Communication provides the information individuals and group need to make decision by transmitting the data to identify and evaluate alternative choice.

Source: Robbins & Judge (2011, pp. 376-377)

3) The Communication Process

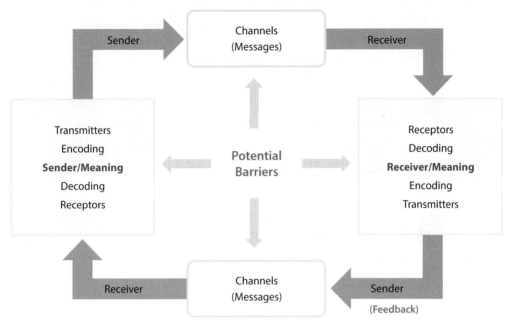

Source: Slocum & Hellriegel (2011, p. 257)

4) Direction of Communication

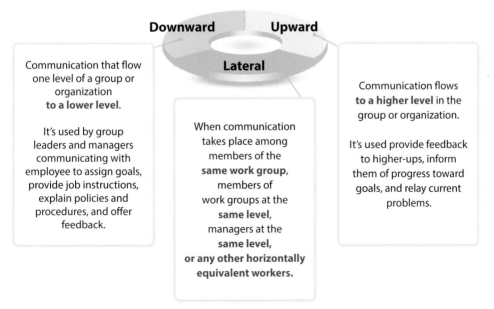

Downward

Communication that flow one level of a group or organization **to a lower level.**

It's used by group leaders and managers communicating with employee to assign goals, provide job instructions, explain policies and procedures, and offer feedback.

Lateral

When communication takes place among members of the **same work group,** members of work groups at the **same level,** managers at the **same level, or any other horizontally equivalent workers.**

Upward

Communication flows **to a higher level** in the group or organization.

It's used provide feedback to higher-ups, inform them of progress toward goals, and relay current problems.

Source: Robbins & Judge (2011, pp. 378-380)

4. Conflict

1) A Definitions of Conflict and conflict management

Slocum & Hellriegel (2011, p. 386)

Conflict is a process in which one party (person or group) perceives that its interests are being opposed or negatively affected by another party.

Conflict management refers to the diagnostic processes, interpersonal styles, and negotiation strategies that are designed to avoid unnecessary conflict and reduce or resolve excessive conflict.

Slocum & Hellriegel (2011, p. 386)

2) Primary Levels of Conflict in Organization

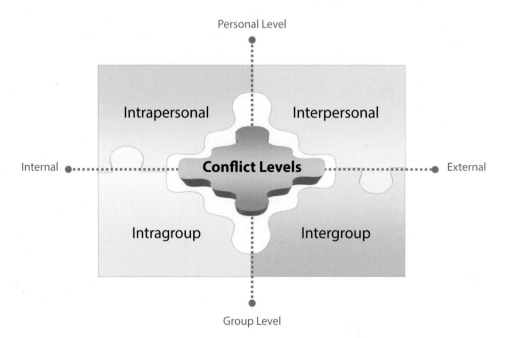

① Personal Level

Intrapersonal Conflict

▶ Intrapersonal conflict occurs within an individual and usually involves some form of goal, cognitive, or affective conflict.
▶ Three basic types of intrapersonal goal conflict
→ Approach-approach conflict, Avoidance-avoidance conflict, Approach-avoidance conflict

▶ Interpersonal conflict occurs when two or more individuals perceive that their attitudes, behaviors, or preferred goals are in opposition.
▶ Source of interpersonal conflict
→ Role conflict, Role ambiguity

Interpersonal Conflict

Source: Slocum & Hellriegel (2011, pp. 388-389)

② Group Level

Intragroup Conflict

▶ Intragroup conflict refers to disputes among some or all of a group's members, which often affect a group's dynamics and affectiveness.

▶ Intergroup conflict refers to opposition, disagreements, and disputes between groups or teams.
▶ Source of intergroup conflict
→ Perceived goal incompatibility, Perceived differentiation, Task interdependency, Perceived limited resources

Intergroup Conflict

Source: Slocum & Hellriegel (2011, pp. 389-391)

3) Conflict-Handling Styles

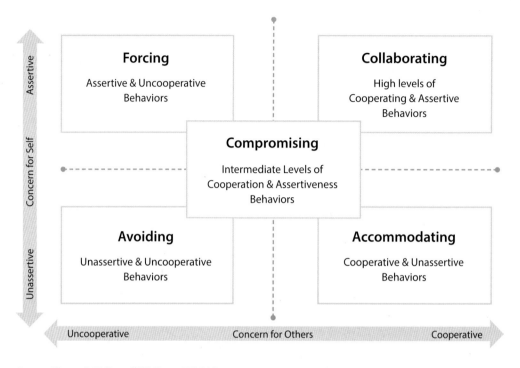

Source: Slocum & Hellriegel (2011, pp. 392-396)

5. Human Resource Development

1) A Definition of HRD

Werner & DeSimone (2006, p. 5)

A set of systematic and planned activities designed by an organization to provide its members with the opportunities to learn necessary skills to meet current and future job demands.

HRD is any process or activity that, either initially or over the long term, has the potential to develop adults' work-based knowledge, expertise, productivity and satisfaction, whether for personal or group/team gain, or for the benefit of an organization, community, nation or, ultimately, the whole of humanity.

Mclean & Mclean (2001, p. 10)

Sambrook & Stewart (2007, p. 8)

HRD is quite a complex subject. The curriculum is not easy to define as the subject continues to evolve and to adopt different concepts. HRD is clearly concerned with professional practice and so needs to be open to and reflective of the context.

2) Primary HRD Functions

Human Resource Development = Individual Development + Career Development + Organization Development

219

① Individual Development

DeSimone & Werner (2012, pp. 19-20, 554)

The process of building an individual's skill or competencies over time. Organizations often offer career counselors to facilitate the process of individual development. The individual development assists individual employees in assessing their competencies and goals in order to develop a realistic career plan. Outputs include individual assessment sessions, workshop facilitation, and career guidance.

② Career Development

DeSimone & Werner (2012, p. 400)

An ongoing process by which individuals progress through a series of stages, each of which is characterized by r relatively unique set of issues, themes, and tasks.

③ Organization Developmentt

DeSimone & Werner (2012, p. 479)

The systemwide application and transfer of behavioral science knowledge to the planned development, improvement, and reinforcement of the strategies, structures, and processes that lead to organization effectiveness.

The process of enhancing the effectiveness of an organization and the well-being of its members through planned interventions that apply behavioral science concepts. It emphasizes both macro-level and micro-level organizational changes.

DeSimone & Werner (2012, p. 556)

3 From Theory to Practice

1. Agency Analysis

Korea Airports Corporation (KAC)

Korea Airports Corporation was established in 1980 to carry out construction, management and operation of airports and to manage air transportation efficiently. As an organization specializing in airport management, KAC manages and operates total of 14 airports in Korea including Gimpo, Gimhae, Jeju, Daegu, Muan, Cheongju, and Yangyang international airport. KAC also manages the Area Control Center, 10 VOR/TACs and Korea Civil Aviation Training Center (www.airport.co.kr).

KAC plays a key role as the control tower of domestic airports in Korea. Nonetheless, there are issues that hinder the effective management of the corporation. The distance from the central office of KAC and other domestic airport causes communication gap between the top management and the subordinate employees. In order to address the issue, the CEO conducts a periodic visit and meeting through the "creation and communication workshop with CEO."The management and staffs of each domestic airport were given the chance to strategize and talk with the CEO. Also, KAC operate 'CEO mailbox', and 'Discussion Square' as well as 'CEO workshop'. Through these programs, KAC enhance its internal communication system between the top management and employees and easily resolve conflicts in the organization.

Discussion Questions on Agency Case

1   Define the terms "communication" and "conflict." How do they relate to each other?

2   What norms or roles are likely to develop in groups? Explain how this occurs.

3   How does group context and structure affect group outcomes?

4   What is a communication structure and how might it affect the motivation of an individual? Use examples in your response.

5   Is conflict a negative or positive phenomenon? Explain.

Class Exercises

1   In what ways do individuals affect group behavior? In what ways do groups affect individual behavior?

2   What are the advantages and disadvantages of groups?

3   In what ways is effective communication more challenging to managers of public organizations compared to their private sector counterparts?

4   What is the manager's task with regard to conflict? In what ways does the public sector context complicate conflict management?

5   What communications distortions are likely to occur in public bureaus?

6   Explain the various approaches to group decision making including: brainstorming, T-groups, nominal groups, and the Delphi techniques.

2. Research Notes

Work Motivation and Social Communication among Public Managers

This article tests hypotheses about the effects of two types of work motivation (i.e. intrinsic motivation and extrinsic motivation) and four types of social communication on three important work dispositions (i.e. job involvement, red tape, and perceived organizational effectiveness) among 790 managers employed in public agencies in the states of Illinois and Georgia. The results show that intrinsic motivation is significantly associated with public managers' job involvement, perceptions of red tape, and organizational effectiveness. Also, certain types of organizational communication and mentoring socialization are closely related to the outcomes. The results of cross-interaction effects between motivation and communications on outcome variables support the SDT prediction that when public managers are more involved with different types of social communication behaviors, the relationship between extrinsic motivation and three outcome variables becomes more pronounced. That is, communication in public agencies provides more autonomy and discretion for extrinsically motivated public managers, thus leading to more positive organizational dispositions.

Research Framework

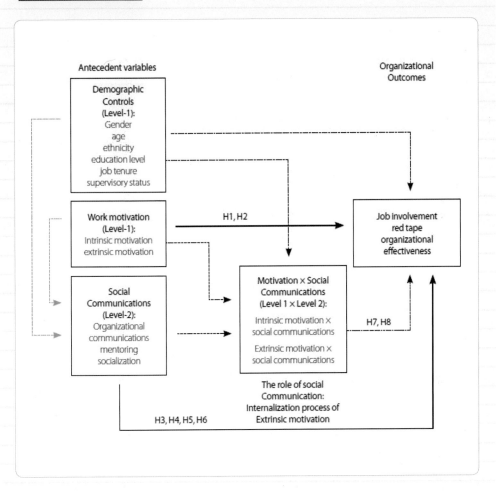

Source: Park & Rainey (2012)

The Effects of Personnel Reform Systems
on Georgia State Employees' Attitudes
: An Empirical Analysis from a Principal-Agent
Theoretical Perspective

In order to maximize the value of human resources, today' reformers have abandoned traditional merit systems, calling instead for public personnel management systems based on a set of new principles known as managerialism. The study at hand, conceived within a principal–agent theoretical framework and using a confirmatory factor analysis (CFA), a hierarchical regression model and a structural equation model (SEM), probed four personnel reform effects in the state of Georgia: (1) a monetary incentive system (i.e. a merit pay system); (2) a performance monitoring system (i.e. a performance appraisal system); (3) a knowledge incentive system (i.e. a training and development system); and (3) a discretionary controlling system (i.e. an at-will system). The research findings indicate that all four personnel reform systems are directly and indirectly associated with organizational consequences. Among these effects, discretionary controlling and performance monitoring systems are most salient and are most effective at enhancing the level of an agent's work motivation and job satisfaction as well as decreasing their turnover intentions. Implications and limitations of this research are also discussed.

Research Framework

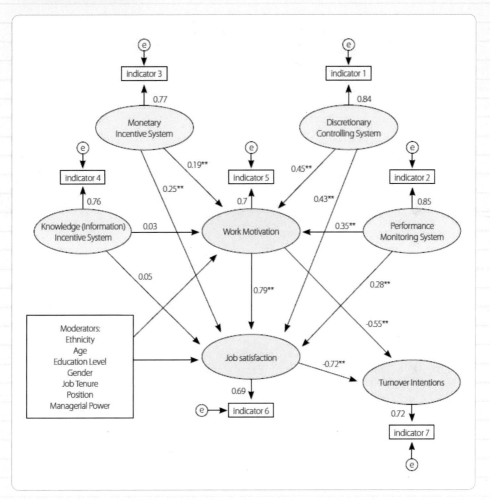

Source: Park (2010)

People

Framework

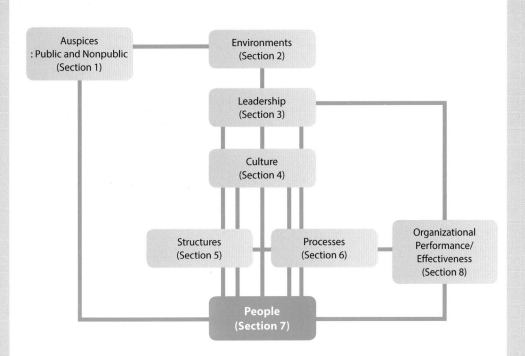

Source: Park, S. M. (2013). *Public Management: A Research Handbook*.
Daeyoung Moonhwasa Publishing Company.

Keyword

- Motivation
- Intrinsic Motivation
- Extrinsic Motivation
- Intrinsic Reward
- Extrinsic Reward
- Public Service Motivation
- Rational PSM
- Affective PSM
- Norm-Based PSM
- Self-Determination Theory

- Content Theory
- Process Theory
- Needs Hierarchy
- Theory X and Theory Y
- Two Factor Theory
- Job Characteristic Theory
- Equity Theory
- Expectancy Theory
- Social Learning Theory
- Goal Setting Theory

Role Play Simulation

1. Play One's Role as a Public Administrator

The Very Capable Jerk

The situation:

You have been asked to consult with a module manager in a public service center of the Social Security Administration. A module is a group of about forty workers who work together in processing claims for social security coverage (that is, requests for the beginning of payments, or other services such as changes and information). A module has all the specialists needed to process a claim from beginning to end—claims authorizers, benefits authorizers, file clerks, and typists or word processors. Each module has a module manager (hereafter, MM) and two assistant module managers (AMMs), who lead and manage the team of workers in the module.

The MM, Joan, has a serious concern about one of the AMMs, Joe. Joe is very intelligent, talented, and younger than most AMMs. As far as his knowledge of the work and technical details is concerned, he is extremely promising and has excellent prospects to move up to become MM and then move on up beyond that. Joe, however, is arrogant in his dealings with the workers in the module. He talks down to people and treats them curtly and rudely. He behaves as if he deserves more special treatment and attention than the module members because he is an AMM. On the other hand, Joe also takes some stands and actions that are not necessarily bad or unjustified.

Following are some incidents that have occurred:

One of the file clerks arrives late fairly often. Joe has begun to confront her very aggressively, in front of the other members of the module, criticizing her for arriving late. He has initiated disciplinary action against her. Some other members of the module have pointed out to Joe and Joan that the file clerk is a young single mother with a lot of personal problems. Her brother was recently shot to death in a street fight, apparently drug related. Her child is sick a lot and she has problems getting good child care. Joe, however, insists on going forward with the disciplinary action, saying he cannot let a person arrive late regularly without being unfair to those who do arrive on time. Besides, he says, it is essentially illegal for him not to take action. Joan has to decide whether to intervene in the disciplinary action or let it go through.

Joan is concerned about Joe's effect on motivation and work satisfaction in the module. He speaks very condescendingly to module members who make mistakes, acting as if he is a lot smarter than they are—which is often true, in a sense. Joan arranged for a weekend retreat, during which the group went through some team development exercises with a consultant. Throughout the retreat and the exercises, Joe had a sneer on his face, and made sarcastic comments about the time the group was wasting on "touchy-feely nonsense."

The members of the module have group meetings to discuss problems and changes. Joe has gotten up and walked out of a couple of these meetings, acting impatient with the discussion. He often frowns and rolls his eyes as members of the group are speaking. After the most recent of these incidents, the other AMM, who is excellent as a person and a manager, has told Joan that she is considering asking to transfer to another module or position because Joe is so unpleasant to work with, and because she feels that Joe is damaging morale in the module so badly that it is disrupting the work of the module.

Joan needs to make decisions about Joe:

Joan has to prepare a performance evaluation for Joe, of course. This will strongly affect his chances to move to higher positions. Also, the director of the center is forming a task force to plan and carry out an important change in work processes for the entire center. He has heard that Joe really knows his stuff, and has asked Joan what she thinks of having Joe appointed as either head of this task force or assistant head. (Joe minds his manners and behaves well in meetings when superiors from outside the module are present).

Joan is very impressed with Joe's intelligence and ability. Joe does have a likeable side that often shows. She also knows that Joe's wife has a long-term serious illness and is facing a series of operations at present, and that one of his children was seriously disabled in an accident two years ago. Joe often talks about being bored in his present position and wanting to move up or to somewhere where he can have more variety and responsibility. Joan wants to support and help Joe, and loathes the idea of having to confront him now with a bad evaluation and with the news that she has not supported his appointment to the task force. She has had a number of talks with Joe about his undesirable behavior and attitudes. She has tried to be very positive, praising his capabilities, telling him she really wants him to succeed, and pointing out that he has opportunities to move up. She urges him to show the good side she sees in him, but says that he needs to change. She has never really come down on him with a bad evaluation. In these discussions, Joe sits quietly with a slight smirk on his face, leaves the discussion without saying anything, and pouts for a day or so. The discussions have shown no effect on his behaviors. She is trying to decide what to do next. One possibility in addition to a bad evaluation is to begin the process of trying to have Joe demoted from AMM.

Source: The case was written by Dr. Hal G. Rainey

Warm-Up Questions

As you read and think about the motivation theories and work-related attitudes that we will cover, consider the following case, and the following questions:

1   What different perspectives on the case would the different theories take? What would they emphasize and point to as most important? What kinds of solutions or alternatives would they suggest?

2   Can you see gaps or weaknesses in the different theories, that come out in trying to apply them to the case? Are some of the concepts and theories more useful for this case than others?

3   What would you advise Joan to do about Joe? Can you ground any of your advice in the theories or ideas about motivation that we cover in the readings and class discussion?

Source: The discussion questions were based on the case written by Dr. Hal G. Rainey

2. Play One's Role as a Government Reformer

Let's suppose you are the newly appointed manager of the Human Resource Management Strategy Office under the Ministry of Public Management in Korea. In your courtesy call meeting with the Minister, he briefed you with the important organizational challenges and the need to boost employee's public service motivation. As your first assignment in the office, the Minister sent you a memorandum via email directing your office to design a program that gears towards enhancing employees' public service motivation. Please read the memorandum for the whole details of the directives and let's try to comply with the order of the Minister

From Minister Sup-Jong Cho (minsiter_mpm@korea.com) You moved this message to its current location.

Sent Monday, May 22, 2015 3:34:29 PM

To HRM Strategy Office (hrmso_mpm@korea.com)

2 attachment | Download all as zip (1234.0 KB) Plan for Enhancing the Public Service Motivation Program.docx (698.0 KB) Looking for a Promotion? Pure Motivations Produce the Best Results.docx (536.0 KB)

View online

MEMORANDUM-MPM0004

TO: The Manager, Human Resource Management Strategy Office (HRMSO)

RE: Enhancing the Public Service Motivation Program

FROM: The Minister, Ministry of Public Management

DATE: 22 May 2015

Our great motivation as a public servant is always anchored on the call for public service. Without any doubt, government employees must possess high degree of ethics and devotion to public welfare compared to private sector employees. It sounds alarming but, the reality about the Korean public employees is already showing us a decreasing pattern of ethics, public spiritedness, and intrinsic motivation.

We need to arrest this depressing problem, if not, will cause further damage both to the organization (i.e., organizational performance, transparency, and responsibility) likewise to the individual employee (i.e., job satisfaction and organizational commitment). It is our role not to keep mum and blind on these patent behavioral flaws.

Thus, 2-weeks from now, I would like you to produce a policy memorandum on "Enhancing the Public Service Motivation" that must include answers to the following general questions:

a. What might be the idiosyncratic characteristics of motivation in the public sector compared to the private sector?
b. To what extent do you think either public service motivation or public sector motivation is more influential than the other for Korean public managers and employees?
c. For Korean bureaucrats, what would be the main issues in the future to effectively activate, cultivate, and maintain work motivation?
d. What do you think are the possible problems that may arise from such characteristics?

After ministerial level deliberation on your policy memo, we are going to submit it to the President for its adoption and immediate implementation.

For your immediate action and compliance.

Attached File 1: Problem-Based Learning (PBL)

Plan for Enhancing the Public Service Motivation Program

	Step	Contents		
1	Environments/ Conditions/ Backgrounds	Please explain the situation briefly.		
2	Problem Definition	In your own perspective, please be as specific as possible when pointing out the problem.		
3	Actual Case Studies	Please explain by giving specific examples (Newspaper articles, news clips, or Interviews)		
4	Finding Alternatives	Possible Solutions	Merits/Pros in a Korean Context	Demerits/Cons in a Korean Context
		①		
		②		
		③		
5	The Best Solution	Why did you choose this alternative as the best solution? What are the expected effects and potential contribution?		

Attached File 2

Looking for a Promotion?
Pure Motivations Produce the Best Results

A new study of West Point cadets finds those driven by purely internal motivations were the most likely to succeed.

What motivates someone to do the best possible job, and ultimately enjoy a successful, satisfying career? Is it an internal pull—a sense that one's work is significant and satisfying—or a desire for the perks that accompany success, such as money and status?

A large body of research points to the first answer. While acknowledging that, it's easy to assume that adding a few extrinsic motives to your intrinsic ones will only strengthen your ambition and determination. But in fact, the opposite appears to be true. ...

... It found those who achieved common markers of career achievement, such as being selected for promotions, were those motivated by purely by such internal factors as love of the job and commitment to national service.

"In real life, people bring multiple motives to almost any course of action," a research team led by Amy Wrzesniewksi of Yale University writes in the Proceedings of the National Academy of Sciences. "Our results demonstrate that instrumental motives can weaken the positive effects of internal motives in real-world contexts." ...

... The key result: "Following their entry into the Army, officers who entered

West Point with stronger (externally driven) motives were less likely to be considered for early promotion, and to stay in the military following their mandatory period of service—even if they also held internally based motives."

This confirms a 1994 theory that, under certain circumstances, external factors can "crowd out" one's internal motivations. If a job doesn't prove to be as glamorous or as lucrative as you had hoped, it can dampen that internal fire that was your original motivation. ...

Source: The information contained in this article was extracted from
"Pacific Standard (2014.07.01)" by Tom Jacobs

2 Theory Synopsis

Motivation is "an umbrella concept that captures the psychological forces that direct, energize, and maintain action" (Grant, 2008). Motivating employees to be both positive and effective in performing their work remains a crucial challenge for managers; selecting, retaining, and managing highly motivated people are primary human resource (HR) functions. As Robert Behn (1995) suggested, one of the "big questions"in the public human resource management is on how to enhance employees work motivation to increase job and organizational performance;increase effectiveness at the micro-level as well as ultimately pursuing social purposes at the macro-level (Behn, 1995).

From a managerial standpoint, employees and manager's work motivation is one of the determining factors of organizational development and success. That is, work motivation is directly linked to an employee's perceptions and behaviors, which in turn reflects how well the manager oversees employees. Public managers and supervisors set the example when it comes to employee motivation. Once a supervisor or personnel manager is motivated to do a good job, their behaviors tend to transfer over to the employees they manage. Public managers and supervisors play the role of leader when it comes to employee motivation.

Section 7 introduces and highlights the extensive and relevant theories and practices of motivation, work attitudes, and incentives. These concepts are regarded as essential components of effectively managing human behaviors in organizations. Specifically, this section clarifies the best way to understand the importance of motivation in public organizations, as well as to define motivation theories and apply them to public organizations. Motivation is what causes people to behave as they do - internal and external forces that initiate behavior and determine its form, direction, intensity and duration. In regard to the themes provided in this section, for example, readers might ask such questions as how can public managers motivate public employees (and citizens, too) to pursue important public purposes with intelligence and energy? We could argue that motivation in the public sector is aimed at the achievement of public purposes. In this regard, work motivation is in essential because it enhances our experience at work. If we are highly motivated, we can influence others in a constructive way and we can make better career choices.

1. Motivation and Public Management

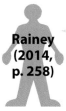

**Rainey
(2014,
p. 258)**

Human motivation is fundamental topic in the social science, and people's motivation to work is similarly a basic topic in the field or organizational behavior. The basic research and theory provide no conclusive science of motivation.

Motivation in public organizations is also greatly affected by the public sector environment. The effects of this environment require public managers to posses an distinctive knowledge of motivation that links OB with political science in way essential to the analysis and practice of management.

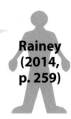

**Rainey
(2014,
p. 259)**

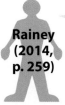

**Rainey
(2014,
p. 259)**

Many analysts and experienced practitioners regard the constraining character of government personnel systems as the critical difference between managing in the public sector and managing in a private organization.

Managing people in government raises challenges very different from those faced by business and nonprofit organization. Another side argues that government differs little from business in matters of motivation.

**Rainey
(2009,
p. 245)**

2. The Context of Motivation in Public Organizations

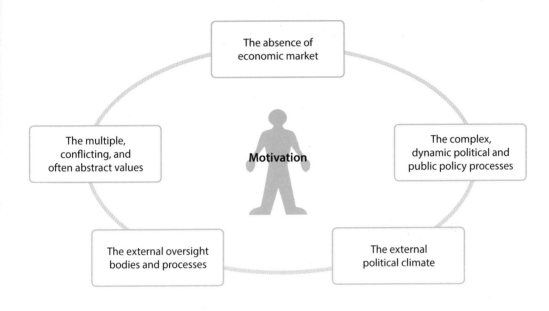

Source: Perry & Porter (1982)

3. The Concept of Motivation

Rainey (2009, p. 263)

Work motivation refers to a person's desire to work hard and **work well**, and to the **arousal, direction**, and **persistence** of effort in work settings.

Motivation techniques are commonly used in all sectors.
cf) Job Choice Motivation
cf) Public / Private Sector Motivation

Rainey (2009)

Slocum & Hellriegel (2011, p. 158)

The **forces acting** on or within a person that cause the person to behave in s specific, goal-directed manner.

The processes that account for an individual's **intensity, direction,** and **persistence** of effort toward attaining a goal.

Robbins & Judge (2011, p. 239)

4. Measuring and Assessing Motivation

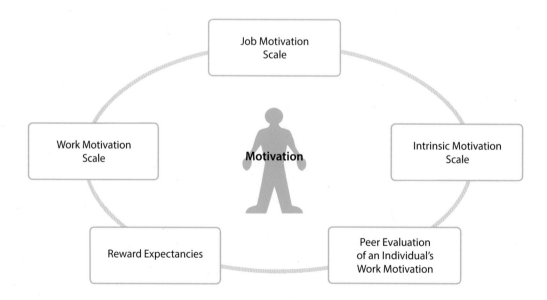

Source: Rainey (2014, pp. 264-265)

5. Rival Influences on Performance

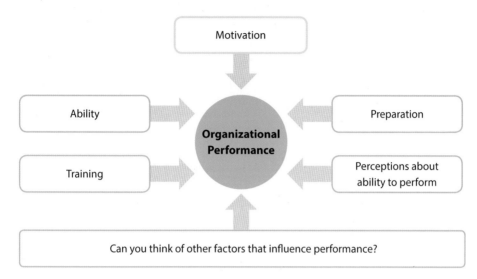

Source: Rainey (2014, p. 267)

6. Type of Incentives

1) Extrinsic Rewards vs. Intrinsic Rewards

Extrinsic Rewards

Rewards extrinsic
to the individual,
part of the job situation,
given by others

Intrinsic Rewards

Rewards intrinsic
to the individual and
stemming directly from
job performance itself,
which satisfy
higher-order needs
such as self-esteem
and sdlf-actualization

Source: Lawler (1971), Rainey (2009, p. 256)

2) Type of Extrinsic Reward

Material   **Purposive**

Solidary

These are tangible rewards; that is, reward that have a monetary value or can easily be translated into ones that have
: wages, salaries, tangible fringe benefits

Solidary rewards are basically intangible; that is, the reward has no monetary value and cannot easily be translated into one that has.
: rewards as socializing, congeniality, the sense of group membership, and identification, the status resulting from membership

Purposive, like solidary, incentives are intangible, but they derive in the main from the stated ends of the association rather than from the simple act of associating. These inducements are to be found in the suprapersonal goals of the organization.
: enactment of law, elimination of corruption

Source: Clark & Wilson (1961, pp. 134-136)

7. The Motive for Public Service

Rainey (2009, p. 266)

The topic of challenging work in the public service and of motives for pursuing it brings us to the motive mentioned in discussions of why people want to work for government – the service ethic, the desire to serve the public, or as researchers on this topic now sometimes refer to it, **P**ublic **S**ervice **M**otivation.

In general, research is consistent with the finding that public managers express a greater motivation to serve the public.

Rainey (2009)

8. Public Service Motivation

1) A Definition of Public Service Motivation

Character	PSM is regarded as a specific sub-type of intrinsic work motivation in the public sector
Perry & wise (1990)	An individual's predisposition to respond to Motives grounded primarily or uniquely in public institutions and organizations
Rainey & Steinbauer (1999)	A general altruistic motivation to serve the interests of a community of people, a state, a nation, or humankind

Public Service Motivation

2) Dimensions of Public Service Motivation

Rational　　**Affective**

Norm-Based

Attraction to Public Policy-Making Process

- Participate in policy making
- Identify important public policy
- Support particular interests

Commitment to Public Interest and Civic Duty

- Calling to public service
- Loyalty and duty toward government
- Derive to pursue social equity

Compassion & Self-Sacrifice

- Commitment to a policy due to its social importance
- Patriotism or benevolence

Source: Perry & Wise (1990)

247

9. Self-Determination Theory

1) Key Elements of SDT

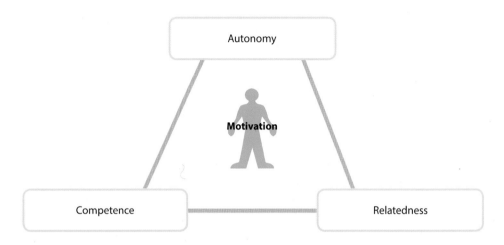

Source: Ryan & Deci (2000)

2) Characteristics of SDT

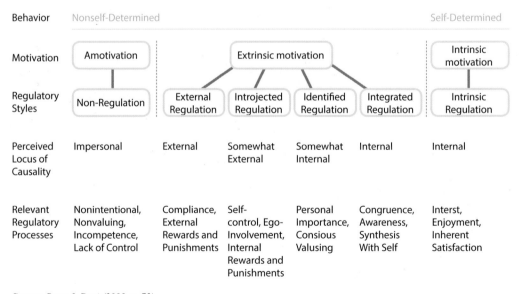

Behavior	Nonself-Determined					Self-Determined
Motivation	Amotivation	Extrinsic motivation				Intrinsic motivation
Regulatory Styles	Non-Regulation	External Regulation	Introjected Regulation	Identified Regulation	Integrated Regulation	Intrinsic Regulation
Perceived Locus of Causality	Impersonal	External	Somewhat External	Somewhat Internal	Internal	Internal
Relevant Regulatory Processes	Nonintentional, Nonvaluing, Incompetence, Lack of Control	Compliance, External Rewards and Punishments	Self-control, Ego-Involvement, Internal Rewards and Punishments	Personal Importance, Consious Valusing	Congruence, Awareness, Synthesis With Self	Interst, Enjoyment, Inherent Satisfaction

Source: Ryan & Deci (2000, p. 72)

10. Theories of Work Motivation

1) Content Theory vs. Process Theory

Content Theories		Process Theories
Concerned with analyzing the **particular needs, motives,** and **rewards** that affect motivation	**Motivation**	Concentrate more on the **psychological** and **behavioral processes** behind motivation, often with no designation of important rewards and motives

Focus on "What"	Focus on "How"
Maslow: Needs Hierarchy McGregor: Theory X and Y Herzberg: Two-Factor Theory Adams: Equity Theory	Vroom: Expectancy Theory Bandura: Social Learning (cognitive) Theory Locke: Goal-Setting Theory

Source: Rainey (2014, pp. 268-269)

2) Content Theories

① Maslow (1954): Needs Hierarchy

Source: Maslow (1954)

Higher Order Needs

Level 5: Self-Actualization Needs ▶ To Achieve Self-Fulfillment

Level 4: Self-Esteem Needs ▶ Sense of Achievement, Confident Recognition, and Prestige

Level 3: Social Needs ▶ For Love, Affection, and Belonging to Social Units and groups

Lower Order Needs

Level 2: Safety Needs ▶ To be Free of the Threat of Bodily Harm

Level 1: Physiological Needs ▶ For Relief from Hunger, Thirst, and Fatigue and for Defense from the Elements

② McGregor (1960) : Theory X and Theory Y

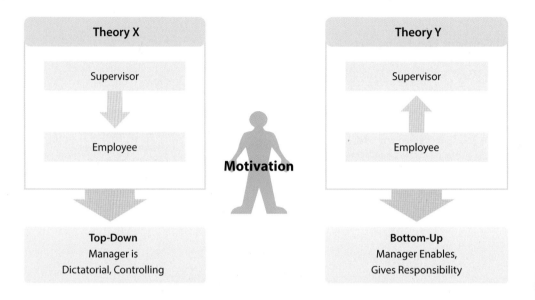

③ Herzberg (1959): Two Factor Theory

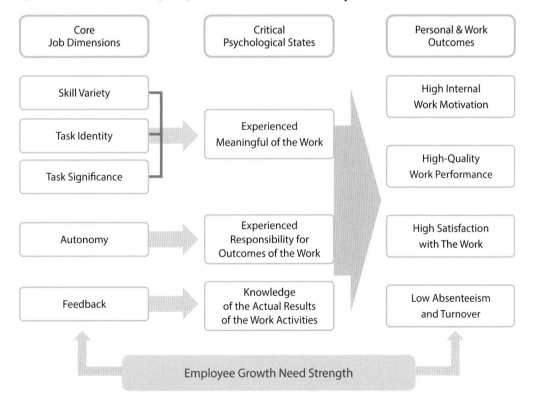

Source: Herzberg (1959, 1968)

④ Hackman & Oldham (1980): Job Characteristics Theory

| Core Job Dimensions | Critical Psychological States | Personal & Work Outcomes |

Skill Variety

Task Identity

Task Significance

Experienced Meaningful of the Work

High Internal Work Motivation

High-Quality Work Performance

Autonomy

Experienced Responsibility for Outcomes of the Work

High Satisfaction with The Work

Feedback

Knowledge of the Actual Results of the Work Activities

Low Absenteeism and Turnover

Employee Growth Need Strength

Source: Hackman & Oldham (1980)

251

3) Process Theories

① Adams (1963): Equity Theory

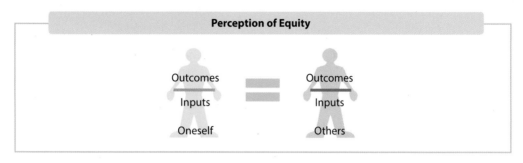

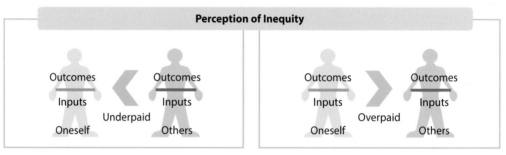

② Vroom (1964): Expectancy Theory / VIE Theory

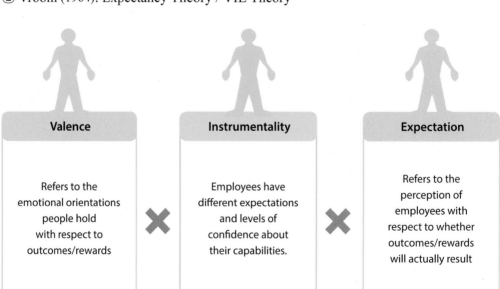

③ Wood & Bandura (1989): Social Learning (Cognitive) Theory

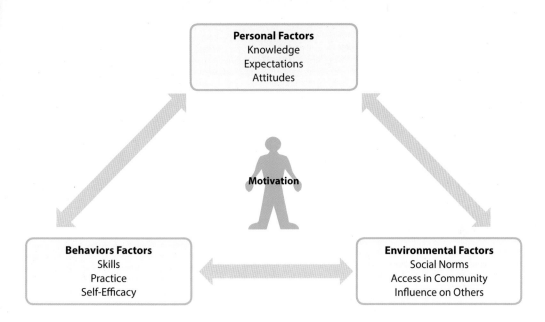

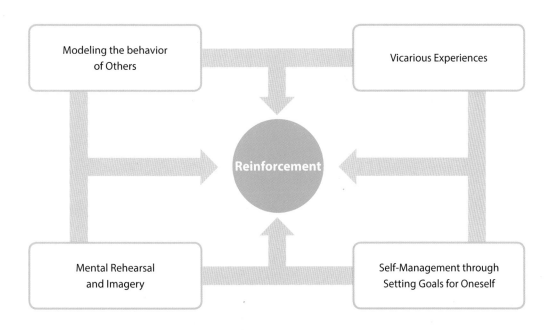

④ Locke & Latham (1990): Goal-Setting Theory

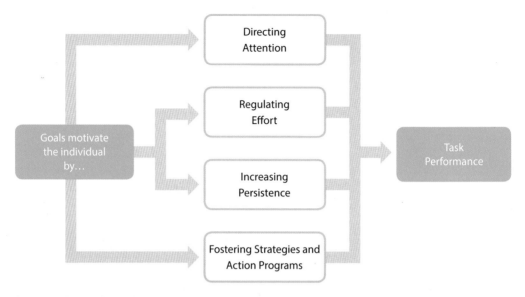

Source: Locke & Latham (1990)

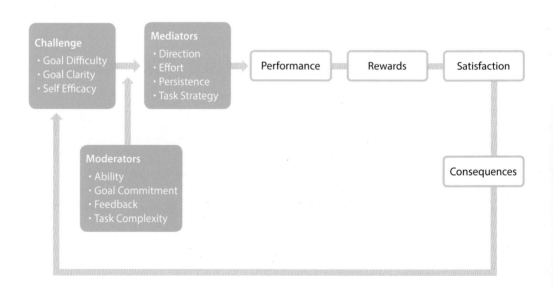

Source: Locke & Latham (1990)

3 From Theory to Practice

1. Agency Analysis

Seodaemun District Office

In many countriesand various organizations—public or private—corruption is always one of the important issues that undermines morality and ethics in the work setting. Worst, corruption can even be a way life that is capable of crippling the whole organizational system. In the public sector, corruption is leading towards a status that totally isolates government and the people. The self-serving corrupt politicians willfully neglected public interest and wittingly or unwittingly make people distrustful on its government and its policy. Various laws, policies, NGOs, private and public institutions were established to focus on the eradication of corruption; however, it appears to be an uphill battle yet to win. At least or at all cost the government should work hard to regain public's trust and stop all forms of corruption in the government service.

To analyze a public sector's efforts in curbing corruption through organizational means, this section will detail specific actions taken in a South Korean district, the Seodaemun District Office.

Seodaemun-gu is one of the growingdistricts in the city of Seoul. The district office has been taking serious efforts to develop well-disciplined public officials by autonomy rather than by heteronomy. This strategic purpose is well manifested in the Seodaemun District's vision and objectives, "Ensure transparent, ethical and open administration." In line with this, Seodaemun-gu Implements various measures and strategies to achieve its aspirations.

The next discussion will center on the analysis of the impacts of various organizational systems in the employees behavior towards corruption. The following organizational systems are: (1) legal system maintenance, (2) integrity mileage system, and (3) integrity education, and integrity-club activity.

Type of Motivation

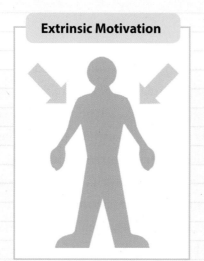

□ Negative Extrinsic Motivation: Legal System Maintenance

Seodaemun District Office enacted local and organizational ordinances to impose discipline among its employees. Fundamentally, the legal intervention is adopted as a coercive measure to hollow out the worsening negative public perception towards its government and rebuild the public trust. Organizational policies, of course in accordance with the fundamental laws and issuances, adhere to the general social policies and promotion of ethical behavior. The local and organizational policy emphasizes three elemental issues; (1) complaints,

(2) compensation, and (3) penalty. The penalty for any culpable violation of the policy is severe such as complete separation from office and forfeiture of benefits. This approach is different to the usual "three strike-out" policy of other organizations; the outright striking out appeals to the Seodaemun-gu's policy.

Organizational policies or legal measures can possess a characteristic that can 'NEGATIVELY' and/or 'EXTRINSICALLY' motivate employees and behave accordingly. Extrinsic motivation can be observed when a person is motivated to perform a behavior in order to earn a reward or avoid a punishment. This motivation can either be in a negative or positive posture. If positive extrinsic motivators challenges individual to do something and receive a corresponding reward, negative extrinsic motivators does the opposite. It challenges the individual not to do something in order to have the reward.

□ **Positive Extrinsic Motivation: Integrity Mileage System**

Negative motivations through punishment have some effects such as increasing individual stress and decreasingjob satisfaction. Among the programs of Seodaemun district, the 'integrity mileage system' is now affecting people with mileages and following incentives. This system is operated by adding and reducing mileages, which serves as the index of integrity. The organization gives plus mileage to the well-performing and incorruptible employees; and minus mileage to less-performing and corruptible employee base on the following standards: (1) code of conduct for public officials, (2) anticorruption righteous activities, (3) customer satisfaction and their sub-categories.

This Integrity Mileage System is a 'POSITIVE' and 'EXTRINSIC' motivator that provides reward for person's positive behaviors and strengthens his will to be incorruptible.Also, beyond themileage system, the year-end award can consistently induce positive motivation to every employee. In addition, evaluating the group or team as well as the individual, the system allows people to recognize their contribution to the efficiency and effectiveness of their group.

□ **Intrinsic Motivation: Education and Club Activity**

Both legal system maintenance and integrity mileage system are extrinsic motivations. Extrinsic motivation can superficially encourage members in the organization, but cannot totally influence attitudes or individual internal values. If the intention does not concur with the ostensible expression, the probability of dissatisfaction might be aggravated. Organizational dissatisfaction can bring about low performance. In the instant case, the impact would come be from organizational integrity, or the very end, organizational secession. Therefore, the organization must try to harmonize organizational culture and individual values. That is, there is a need to induce 'INTRINSIC' motivation.

Seodaemun District Office conducts integrity education and integrity club to foster incorruptible characteristic public officials. Integrity Education is a training program required for all employees; over 15 hours is required for each employees to complete the program. It is also worthy to note that, this is not a simple training program, but also integrate debating classes. About 30 people participate on debating with various issues that calls for the promotion of government integrity. This training education strategy enhances the power of delivering information through grouping and helps participants critically think about integrity. Moreover, Seodaemun District Office started in 2013 the Integrity-Club Activity. The club is called 'O2', which means, 'be transparent again today.' Club O2 initiates diverse campaign activities such as campaign for the proliferation of a clean culture, formulate goals and implement activities to materialize the same. The club is an employee-led organization. Its creation is a spontaneous outcome of motivated employees who wants to have an organizational movement towards clean and honest public governance. This activity shows that sometimes people earn more motivation through volunteerism. Same principle enunciated in the 'self-determinant theory'. Indeed, intrinsic motivation helps to inspire employees, boost their individualvolition to realize the vision, mission, and goal of real public service, and settle with the fundamental and ultimate culture for the integrity.

Discussion Questions on Agency Case

1   Do you think there are stereotypes about motivation of public employees? What are they? Do you think they are true?

2   What is the difference between extrinsic and intrinsic incentives? Provide examples of both in the context of your place of work (or your motivation to perform well at school).

3   What is public service motivation? How does Perry define and measure it? Do you consider this an adequate definition and a universal measure that could be applicable and acceptable in the Korean context?

4   Identify the five core dimensions and three critical psychological states in the Job Characteristics Model and explain the causal path suggested by Hackman and Oldham using the agency case above.

Class Exercises

1 Consider your own membership in an organization. Make three lists of factors: those that motivated you to join, those that motivate you to maintain your membership, and those that may prompt you to disassociate yourself from the organization. Do the same factors apply to all three cases? Are your responses (or reasoning for your responses) consistent with what scholars (Barnard, 1938; March & Simon, 1958) have said on the subject of motivation, and more specifically on the factors relevant to joining organizations and maintaining memberships?

2 Herbert Simon made the following statement with regard to incentives: "Everything… about economic rewards applies equally to privately owned, nonprofit, and government owned corporations. The opportunity for, limits on, the use of rewards to motivate activities towards organizational goals are precisely the same in all three kinds of organization (1995, p. 283)." Drawing on key readings and ideas in this chapter and in previous chapters, develop a counter argument. If possible, use examples and/or provide evidentiary support for your position.

3 Interview a person working in a public organization, a private organization, and a non-profit organization to find out what motivated them to seek their jobs. Responses can be compared to research in public service motivation cited in this chapter.

2. Research Notes

Antecedents, Mediators, and Consequences of Affective, Normative, and Continuance Commitment : Empirical Tests of Commitment Effects in Federal Agencies

This study examines the constructs and the effects of three subdimensions of federal employees' organizational commitment—affective, normative, and continuance. Using the Merit Systems Protection Board (MSPB) 2000 survey instrument and employing an exploratory and confirmatory factor analysis, multivariate regression, and a structural equation model, the authors empirically test and measure (a) the dimensionality of the three commitment constructs, (b) how and to what extent antecedent variables would affect the three different commitment variables—affective, normative, and continuance— and (c) how these three commitment values differently influence several outcome variables. The authors confirm that there are three distinctive constructs of commitment to stay in federal agencies and that transformation-oriented leadership (TOL), empowerment, goal clarity, public service–oriented motivation (PSOM), procedural equity perceptions, and objective appraisal systems have direct and indirect effects on the commitment variables. Affective commitment is most significantly and positively associated with these antecedents, and higher affective commitment also has the most significant effect on organizational consequences.

Research Framework

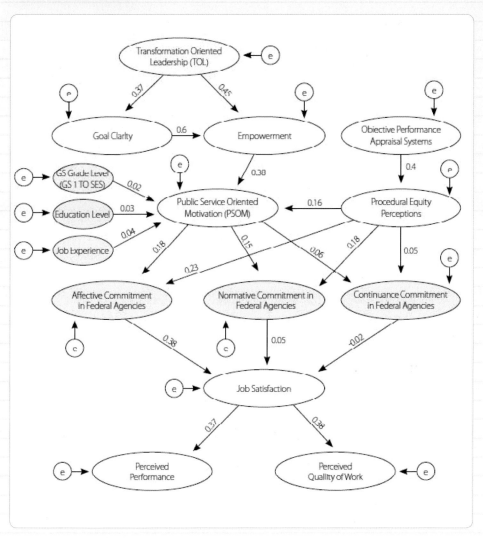

Source: Park & Rainey (2007)

Exploring the Antecedents and Consequences of the Acceptance of Performance Appraisal Systems : The U.S. Federal Case

The main purpose of this study is to investigate the antecedents and onsequences of acceptance by employees of performance appraisal systems (APAS) in U.S. federal agencies. Despite the importance of performance appraisal systems (PAS), a relatively small number of studies have explored the topic. Using data collected through a Merit Systems Protection Board (MSPB) survey in U.S. federal agencies, as well as drawing on different types of management theories and a set of testable research hypotheses, this study examines the relationships among antecedents, APAS, and consequences. Placing APAS as a key mediator in a structural equation model, we hypothesize that APAS among employees is influenced by the effects of mission congruency, adequacy of rewards, and organizational justice perceived by employees. In addition, APAS increases job satisfaction and trust in supervisors among employees. The main findings of this research demonstrate that mission congruency, adequacy of rewards, and organizational justice are positively and directly related to APAS. Among these factors, organizational justice is singled out as the most significant factor for APAS. Further, APAS is positively and directly related to job satisfaction and trust in supervisors among employees. Implications of these findings for both public management theory and practice are provided herein.

Research Framework

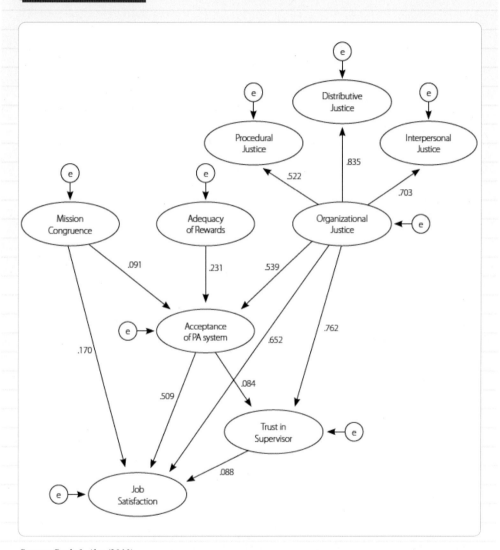

Source: Park & Ahn (2013)

Organizational Performance / Effectiveness

Framework

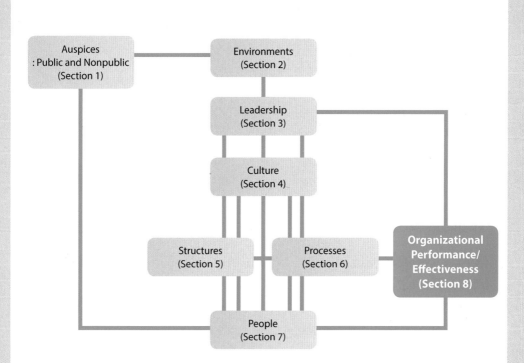

Source: Park, S. M. (2013). *Public Management: A Research Handbook.*
        Daeyoung Moonhwasa Publishing Company.

Keyword

- Organizational Performance
- Organizational Effectiveness
- Total Quality Management
- Reinventing Government Movement
- National Performance Review
- President's Management Agenda
- Goal Approach
- System-Resource Approach
- Participant Satisfaction Models
- Internal Process Approach
- Human Resource and Internal Process Models
- Government Performance Project
- Office Management and Budget Scorecard
- Performance Assessment Rating Tool Scores
- Best Places to Work Index

Role Play Simulation

1. Play One's Role as a Public Administrator

The Move to Best Value in the UK

The new direction of performance management in the United Kingdom is well illustrated by the current local government modernization programme, many elements of which have acted as pilots for the modernization programme in the health services and other parts of government.

The first part of this programme, the 'Best Value' initiative, was introduced in local government in 1997 to replace the much-hated CCT legislation, first as a pilot initiative, then as a statutory duty, from 1 April 2000.

In practice, Best Value means (DETR, 1999a):

■ Every part of the council's budget must be reviewed at least once every five years.
■ Every review must apply the '4Cs' methodology to the service or the cross-cutting issue, which consists of the following steps:
– Challenge the need for the service and the way it is carried out
– Consult with all relevant stakeholders
– Compare the performance of the service with other providers
– Compete –test the competitiveness of the service.

■ As a minimum level of comparison, each authority has to compare its performance with other comparable authorities against each of the 'Best Value performance indicators' (of which there are around one hundred in the case of the largest local authorities). These indicators include some which measure inputs, volume of activity, volume of output, productivity levels, unit costs, number of users, percentage of schoolchildren passing exams at 16 and 18, user satisfaction levels, reliability levels, numbers of complaints and so on –in other words, the whole spectrum from inputs to outcomes and from efficiency to quality.

- Each local authority must publish a plan to improve its performance significantly. Initially, these plans had to ensure that, within five years, each service would reach the performance level which the upper quartile of authorities achieved in 2000. (In 2002 this was amended to give more emphasis to 'stretch targets' agreed by each local authority with government departments across a range of priority issues.)

Warm-Up Questions

1   As you have been informed in this case, in 2000 the UK central government removed the compulsory competitive tendering regime in localgovernment and replaced it with a Best Value approach, in which the quality of services hasto be assessed. If you were a local public official in the UK or other countries, what would you prefer among the main types of performance indicators/standards/outcomes which need to be measured andreported in the public sector? Who cares about these performance measures –and why do you care?

2   How can an organization decide whether its performance management system produces benefits at least as great as the costs it imposes?

3   Discuss how your class, your tutor and your college assess performance – of students, of staff and of the organization as a whole. What are the major limitations in this performance assessment? How could they be tackled?

Source: The discussion questions were based on the case written by Dr. Hal G. Rainey

2. Play One's Role as a Government Reformer

Let's suppose you are the manager of the Performance Management Office (PMO) under the Ministry of Public Management in Korea. The Minister has been doubtful and wary over the acceptability and fairness of the existing performance evaluation system. He has been discussing with your office on possible practical approaches to improve the system. Nonetheless, there are missing links that leads to an incomplete design of a new performance evaluation not until his return from his business trip to Canada. The Minister sent a memorandum via email directing your office to immediately device a new public sector performance evaluation system that will replace the out-dated public organization performance approach. Please read the memorandum for further information regarding the directive.

From   Minister Sup-Jong Cho (minsiter_mpm@korea.com) You moved this message to its current location.

Sent   Thursday, May 22, 2014 3:34:29 PM

To   PM Office (pmo_mpm@korea.com)
2 attachment | Download all as zip (1673.0 KB) Performance Evaluation System Reform Plan.docx (698.0 KB) Performance Management in Canadian Public Agencies: The Federal Case (975.0 KB)
View online

MEMORANDUM-MPM0005

TO: The Manager, Performance Management Office (PMO)
RE: Performance Evaluation System Reform
FROM: The Minister, Ministry of Public Management
DATE: 22 May 2014

The existing performance management system in our country appears to be far behind other nations like Canada. Their system provides a mechanism that ensures sustainable culture of high performance and an assurance of high-quality programs and services for the Canadians.

In my meeting with the Canadian Minister of the Ministry of Public Management and the Manager of the Performance Management Office, I proposed a benchmarking proejcet between Korea's public management system and with that of Canada's system. They generously agreed and handed to me a blueprint of Canada's Performance Management System that can be used for our reform initiatives (see attached file).

Considering our contextual issues and the best practices from other countries like Canada, I hereby direct your office to develop and submit a "Public Performance Evaluation System Plan." I would like you to give a serious attention and provide an elaborate response on the following issues:

a. Determine the similarities and differences between Canada and Korea;
b. What are the main issues of performance management systems of Korea's central agencies?
c. Adopting best practices of Canada, discuss possible issues that may arise and identify ways to resolve these issues;
d. Suggest specific mechanisms to improve Korea's performance management system.

For your immediate action and compliance.

Attached File 1: Problem-Based Learning (PBL)

Performance Evaluation System Reform Plan

	Step	Contents		
1	Environments/ Conditions/ Backgrounds	Please explain the situation briefly.		
2	Problem Definition	In your own perspective, please be as specific as possible when pointing out the problem.		
3	Actual Case Studies	Please explain by giving specific examples (Newspaper articles, news clips, or Interviews)		
4	Finding Alternatives	Possible Solutions	Merits/Pros in a Korean Context	Demerits/Cons in a Korean Context
		①		
		②		
		③		
5	The Best Solution	Why did you choose this alternative as the best solution? What are the expected effects and potential contribution?		

Attached File 2

Performance Management
in Canadian Public Agencies
: The Federal Case

1. Development process of Canadian organizational and individual performance management systems

With the purpose of improving management practices and controls, Canada introduced a performance assessment system in the 1970s. The systematic performance assessment was established when the Treasury Board of Canada announced the assessment policies and established the Evaluation Board in 1997. In Canada, the demand for government's accountability increased due to the financial crisis from 1980s to 1990s and a large scale scandal related to budget projects in the mid 2000; all this were added up to provide an opportunity for Canada to reinforce the performance management in its governance.

In this context, the Canadian government believed that the performance management of the human resources plays the most important role in the organization and its main role was to improve the organizational performance and secure accountability. And the Canadian government established the Performance Management Program for Executives (PMPE) in 1999. It was done to secure the senior government officials' accountability to the government's main policies, programs and people. The emphasis on the government's accountability can be also found in 'Results for Canadians' published in 2000 and 'Managing for Results.' 'Results for Canadians' is based on four management commitment key words; citizen focus, public service values, managing for results, and responsible spending (Treasury Board of Canada Secretariat, 2000). And 'Managing for Results' presents various methods to establish an effective and integrated performance management system based on the four key words mentioned above (President of the Treasury Board, 2000).

The Canadian government's performance of the management system is can be seen to be based on the idea of embodying the vision of modern public service management, as established according to national policy, into a series of Management Expectations. The Treasury Board of Canada Secretariat (TBS) is responsible for carrying out the construction of the Canadian federal government's organizational performance management system and the individual performance management system. The duties of the TBS include: establishing financial, human resource, and administrative policies for government administration, and supervising and checking the implementations of these by each department and organization. In addition, it sets the principles and the direction for performance assessment, develops and delivers guidelines, supervises the implementation of assessment, and reviews the results. In other words, TBS is in charge of the overall management of the performance management system including its development, management, adjustment and supervision; there is no independent organization to assess the different departments by function.

2. Canadian Performance Management System

1) Organizational Performance Management

As discussed above, performance management in Canada has been led by TBS, Canadian budget authority. The organizational performance management is divided into the following: annual department assessment, which assesses each organization and minister, and the meta assessment, which is conducted once every 5 years.

The annual department assessment is based on MAF announced by TBS in 2003 and it takes the form of a self assessment by each department. The main purpose for TBS to introduce MAF was to integrate and adjust the various performance management approaches and turn the public service management vision to rational management expectations. Moreover, MAF contributes to the reinforcement of desirable management in the public service sector by providing an overall integrated model for management and improvement to public service managers.

To achieve this goal, MAF consists of indicators/areas of management and lines of evidence to assess based on the 10 elements, and each assessment item aims to improve the Canadian federal government's administrative management competencies. The assessment indicators of 2011-2012 assessment year (round VIII) assessed 10 elements based on 14 management areas and 53 lines of evidence. Unlike the annual assessment in the form of a self assessment, the once in 5 year meta assessment is carried out by a multinational consulting firm (Pricewaterhouse Coopers LLP). The meta assessment is based on the relevance, success, and cost-effectiveness aspects of MAF assessment.

By reviewing the results of the department assessment and the meta assessment from the overall and the multilateral sides, TBS is improving and developing the assessment indicators every year. As a result, MAF is contributing to the assessment of the work progress and the reinforcement of accountability to management results by managers, vice ministers, and federal administrative organizations by using clear indicators and scales. Moreover, MAF has established a clear connection among the management improvement actions by integrating the basic management framework of previous TBS by modernizing the human resource management, improving service, the integrated risk management, and the modern audit function. The details of Canadian organizational performance management are as follows.

(1) Department Assessment

① Assessment Purpose

The once a year department assessment in the form of a self assessment is carried out based on the following assessment standards and principles provided by TBS; first, a strict and objective assessment; second, an outcome based management focusing on the management results rather than the management capabilities; third, emphasis on the managers' accountability; and fourth, the focus of performance measurement is on the efficiency rather than the effectiveness.

TBS utilizes the results of self assessment in the following areas. First, the results of department assessment provide overall view of the department's efficient performance management. Second, they provide a checklist that enables communication on the priority of work guidelines and management improvement. Third, they provide a groundwork for the assessment for management within the 5 year cycle of payment and management reviews by TBS. Fourth, they are used to facilitate the process of reporting department management plan and performance results to the Parliament. The utility of department assessment system according to MAF can be divided into 4 stages.

The first is the outcome stage. Each department and ministry carries out self assessment based on MAF. Based on the assessment results, recommendations and continuous advice and support for each department and ministry are made . Moreover, putting together and analyzing the results of department assessments provides national and international level administrative management analysis information and public communication information related to MAF. The second is the immediate outcome stage. Due to MAF, it is possible to form consensus on the implementation of management standards, recognize and establish action plans for various administrative management problems of each department and ministry. And it became possible to understand the role of TBS in various administrative management phenomena including the risk elements and provide information on the administrative management phenomena to the Parliament and people. The third is the intermediate outcome stage. MAF made possible the reinforcement of each department and ministry's implementation capabilities to improve the management performance and TBS's competency in providing support and advice to each department and ministry for more effective administrative management. The final one is the ultimate outcome stage. The announcement of MAF and assessment of departments based on MAF improved the quality of administrative management in the federal government and reinforced the government's accountability to people.

② Operation of Assessment System

- Assessment Elements

MAF consists of 10 elements of the framework, including ① public service values, ② governance and strategic directions, ③ learning, innovation and change management, ④ results and performance, ⑤ policy and programs, ⑥ people, ⑦ citizen-focused service, ⑧ risk management, ⑨ stewardship, ⑩ accountability.

In the department assessment, materials are collected through various channels for each assessment area. The sources of evidence consist of survey, documents and plans – submitted by each department and ministry – , reports, performance management agreements, data in the administrative data system, each department and ministry's project management competency assessment and report, and documents submitted by TBS, which is an effort to secure reliability and validity of the assessment.

- Assessment Indicators

The assessment areas and the assessment indicators (based on 2012-2013 assessment data) used are developed based on the 10 elements of accountability model. Until 2010, the assessment elements and areas remained the same; however, from the 2010-2011 assessment year (round VIII), the assessment areas were broken down into 15. The 15 assessment areas were set by emphasizing the interdependent and integrative nature of modern management within the 10 elements. The 15 areas of assessment, set within the 10 elements, all have lines of evidence, each of which consists of sub measures. Based on assessment indicators for 2011-2012 assessment year (round VIII), 14 major assessment areas consist of ① values and ethics, ② managing for Results, ③ citizen-focused service, ④ internal audit, ⑤ evaluation, ⑥ financial management and control, ⑦ management of security, ⑧ integrated risk management, ⑨ people management, ⑩ procurement, ⑪ information management, ⑫ information technology, ⑬ asset management, ⑭ investment planning and management of projects. The line of evidence for each area is shown in <Table 1>.

<Table 1> MAF Assessment Methodology

Area of Management	Line of Evidence	Rate
Values and Ethics	Culture	35%
	Leadership	35%
	Governance	35%
Managing for Results	Quality of the Strategic Outcomes (SO) and Program Activity Architecture (PAA).	15%
	Quality of the Performance Measurement Framework (PMF).	40%
	Quality of Performance Reporting	25%
	Extent to which Management, Resources and Results Structure (MRRS) information is used to support planning and decision making	20%

Citizen-focused Service	Sound Service Management	55%
	Client Service Orientation	20%
	Consideration of Public and Client Views/Needs	25%
Internal Audit	Sustainability	40%
	Performance	60%
Evaluation	Foundations for Quality of Evaluation	50%
	Use of Evaluation	50%
Financial Management and Control	Planning Cycle	10%
	Operations Cycle	50%
	Reporting Cycle	40%
	Sustainability within the Planning	27%
Management of Security	Governance and Planning	-
	Capacity and Processes	-
	Monitoring, Performance Measurement and Reporting	-
	Results	-
	Leadership	-
Integrated Risk Management	Governance and Leadership	10%
	Implementation	65%
	Results and Continuous Improvement	25%
People Management	Employee Engagement	0%
	Executive Leadership	10%
	Diversity and Employment Equity	10%
	Employee Learning	10%
	Performance and Talent Management	10%
	Workload and Workforce Planning Effectiveness	10%
	Staffing	10%
	Official Languages	10%
	Organizational Context	30%

Procurement	Governance, Leadership and Planning	50%
	Capacity, Implementation and Outcomes	50%
	Key Performance Indicator	0%
Information Management	Information Management (IM) Governance	-
	Strategic Planning and Implementation	-
	Practice	-
	Access to Information	-
	Privacy	-
	Access to Information and Privacy (ATIP) Governance and Capacity	-
Information Technology	not assessed in 2011-2012, 2012-2013	-
Asset Management	A real property management framework is supportive of timely, informed real property management decisions	60%
	A materiel management framework is supportive of timely, informed materiel management decisions	40%
Investment Planning and Management of Project	Investment Planning	50%
	Effective Management of Project Resources	25%
	Effective Management of Project Results	25%

Source: Treasury Board of Canada Secretariat Homepage (www.tbs-sct.gc.ca)

(2) Meta Assessment

① Assessment Purpose

To improve the effectiveness, reliability and validity of the department assessment based on MAF, TBS carries out a meta assessment once every 5 years. The meta assessment is carried out by a multinational consulting firm (Pricewaterhouse Coopers LLP) instead of a government organization to secure/ maintain objectivity of the assessment process and results.

② Operation of Assessment System

The basic model of MAF meta assessment is shown in <Figure 1>. The important assessment issues of MAF meta assessment are threefold ; relevance, success, and cost effectiveness of the performance. Four strategic questions are set based on these issues and the assessment questions of each area are 23. The details are as follows.

In the meta assessment, data sources have been diversified to secure validity of the assessment. The materials for assessment consist of document/literature review, interviews with key stakeholders, international comparison, cost survey and analysis, and comparison of revised indicators and scales (measures) by the round.

<Figure 1> MAF Meta Evaluation Framework

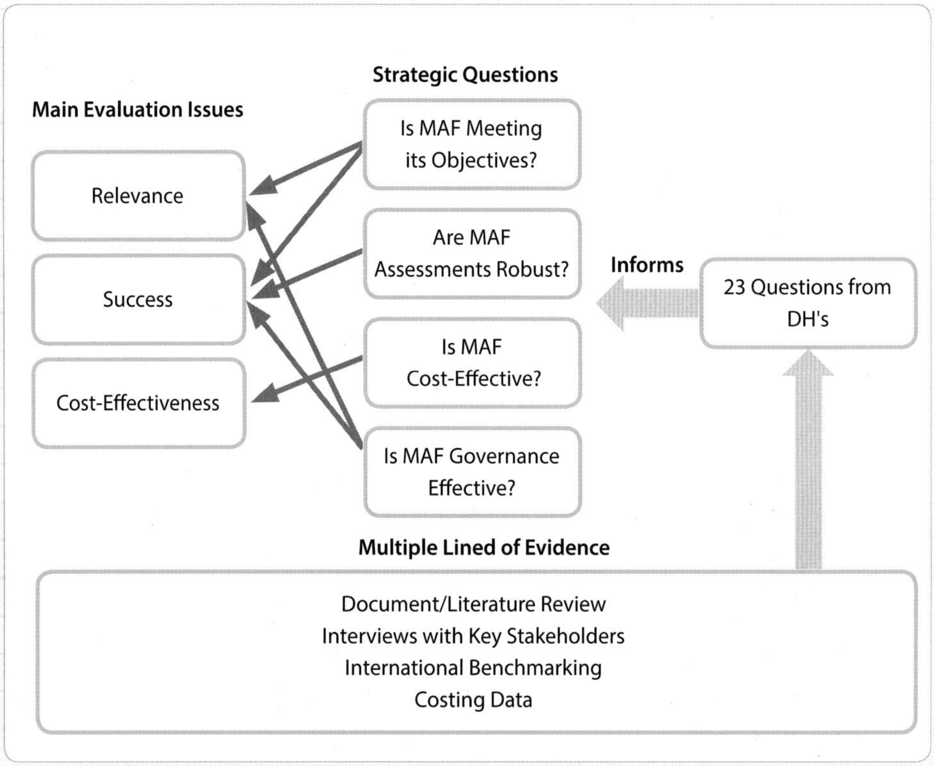

Strategic Questions

Main Evaluation Issues

Relevance

Is MAF Meeting
its Objectives?

Success

Are MAF
Assessments Robust?

Informs

23 Questions from
DH's

Cost-Effectiveness

Is MAF
Cost-Effective?

Is MAF Governance
Effective?

Multiple Lined of Evidence

Document/Literature Review
Interviews with Key Stakeholders
International Benchmarking
Costing Data

Source: Treasure Board of Canada Secretariat (2009b)

2) Individual Performance Management

This chapter examines the current individual performance management system of Canada. The study focuses on the Performance Management Program for Executives (PMPE). PMPE is carried for the following three purposes; first, it is to encourage excellent performance through clear goal setting and strict assessment of performance; second, it aims to recognize and compensate performance; and third, it intends to provide a consistent and fair system of performance management (Treasury Board of Canada Secretariat, 2009a).

The schedule of PMPE consists of 6 stages. From January to March, the responsibility for each department and individual is set and discussed. From April to May, a draft of performance agreement is created. In May, the performance agreement is completed and the compensation for previous year's performance is handled. In June, the payment of performance bonus is reported. From June to July, the performance agreement is evaluated and adjusted. And from August to September, feedback on the year's performance is given.

The process of PMPE can be divided into 5 stages as shown in <Figure 2>. The first is the commitment stage. Performance agreement on policies, programs, management, leadership competencies, and expected results is made. The second stage is the assessment stage. In this stage, the assessment of achieved results as to what is done and important leadership competencies as to how it is done is made. In other words, the assessment of senior government officials considers how it is done as well as what is done. The third stage is the stage of deciding rating. Rating consists of 5 levels; surpassed, succeeded +, succeeded, succeeded -, and did not meet. The fourth stage is the payment/distribution of the performance pay, which consists of economic increase, in-range salary movement, at-risk pay, and bonus. The last stage is the performance feedback stage, which is given in the middle of the year and at the end of the year.

<Figure 2> Performance Management Program for Executive

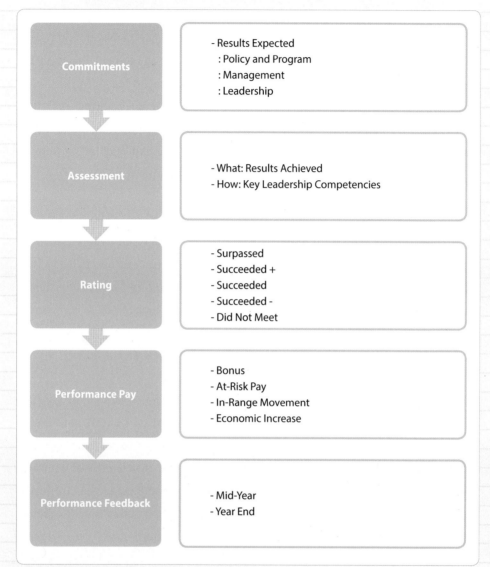

Source: Treasury Board of Canada Secretariat (2009a)

(1) Commitments

The commitment stage is based on the creation of performance agreement and is created based on a mutual understanding of the performance interval expected by the senior government official and his/her immediate supervisor. It consists of 5-6 performance indicators related to policies, programs, management, and leadership.

(2) Assessment

① What

The assessment of results as to what is done consists of three areas: programs and policies, management, and leadership.

- Program and Policy Results

The performance agreement is strategically created based on the organization's project plan. The senior government officials could propose and write their own annual plan and they are required to achieve it through their KSAs. Therefore, the performance agreement process should be outcome-based, and measurable or clearly provable.

- Management Results

The performance plan on special management results is based on the priority of the organization including specific reference work on the human resource management. As a result, the performance agreement is decided according to the organization's priority and by reflecting 1 or 2 areas focusing on the performance cycle.

- Leadership Results

Assessment of the leadership results consists of four core leadership competencies, including values and ethics (serving with integrity and respect), strategic thinking (innovating through analysis and idea), engagement (mobilizing people, organizations partners), and management excellence (delivering through action management, people management, financial manage). All senior government officials are assessed against the expected actions as expressed by the core leadership competencies, and related sub competencies are checked by the level of the performance achievement.

② How

The Canadian government's 'Key Leadership Competencies (2006)' provides information to government employees by separating effective behaviors and ineffective behaviors expected from them. The assessment of core leadership competencies as how to achieve effective behaviors has 4 areas: values and ethics, strategic thinking, engagement, and management excellence. The value and ethics competency is based on integrity and respect. The strategic thinking competency involves innovation through analysis and ideas. The engagement competency involves people, organization, and mobilization of partners. And the management excellence competency involves activity management, human resource management and finance management.

(3) Rating

Rating of performance is decided not only by each senior government official's performance against the performance agreement but also by the scope and the complexity of the problems he/she handles; it is also decided by reflecting how it is achieved as well as what is achieved. Important leadership competencies in the achievement of results are recognized and compensated. In general, the performance assessment area is assessed based on 5 levels; surpassed, succeeded +, succeeded, succeeded -, and did not meet.

Effectiveness of performance management program is proven by the following distribution of the ratios of excellence. The rating of 'surpassed' does not exceed 20% of the total, and the ratings of 'succeeded+' and 'succeeded' do not exceed

65% of the total. The rating of' 'succeeded' does not exceed 10% of the total and the rating of 'did not meet' does not exceed 5% of the total.

(4) Performance Pay

PMPE provides opportunities to get/receive compensation based on performance. The performance pay takes into account the following 4 factors/forms.

① Economic Increase

Economic increase is recommended by Advisory Committee on Senior Level Retention and Compensation and reflects the increase in basic pay. Qualification is decided by the achievement of performance agreement in general. Economic increase can be given even when the performance cannot be assessed but it is not given when the performance agreement is not met.

② In-range Increase

Moving to the maximum level of salary can be achieved through a successful achievement of performance. The regular increase range for successful achievement of performance is within 5% a year, and a higher or lower ratio is decided according to the level of achieved performance goal. In-range salary movement is not given when the expected performance is not achieved.

③ At-risk pay

Single payment of at-risk pay corresponds to the basic pay; it is paid every year based on the level of performance achievement. The total amount of this payment differs according to the level of performance achievement based on the information indicated under each section of the performance assessment. This payment does not increase an individual's basic pay but it is included in the average pay for the calculation of pension. At-risk pay can be given irrespective of the individual's pay range but it is not given when expected performance is not achieved.

④ Bonus

A single payment in the form of a bonus is given in addition to the at-risk pay. when a superior performance of targeted goal is achieved. Like at-risk pay, bonus does not increase an individual's basic pay but it is included in the average pay for the calculation of pension, and it can be given irrespective of the individual's pay range. The types of compensation discussed above can be classified according to the level of performance achievement as shown in <Table 2>.

<Table 2> Performance Pay

Evaluation Results	Economic Increase	In-Range Increase	Lump Sum Performance Award	
			At-Risk Pay	Bonus
Surpassed	O	O	O	O
Succeeded +	O	O	O	X
Succeeded	O	O	O	X
Succeeded -	O	O	O	X
Unable to assess	O	X	X	X
Did not Meet	X	X	X	X

Source: Treasury Board of Canada Secretariat (2009 a)

(5) Performance Feedback

The focus of performance feedback is to grow, share constructive feedback, and include recommendations for the performance reinforcement. One's immediate supervisor provides the performance feedback throughout the performance cycle and focuses on mid-year and year-end assessments at the same time.

Source: This article was written by Sung Min Park and Seona Kim in 2013

2 Theory Synopsis

More important than efficiency in carrying out given tasks were initiatives, imagination and energy in the pursuit of public purposes. Those purposes were political and the administrators charged with responsibility for them, as well as many of their subordinates, had to be politically sensitive and knowledgeable. (Mosher, 1968, pp. 79–80)

Section 8 mainly explains the core components and configuration of organizational performance and effectiveness in the public sector. Most notably, the last decade saw increased efforts to improve government through various performance assessment systems. For example, from the Clinton administration' National Performance Review (NPR), the mantra of making government cost less yet work better evolved to the results-oriented philosophy of the Bush administration. The theory was that managers who were supposedly hampered by stringent rules in human, financial, and management needed freedom to manage in ways that would result in more efficiency and accountability to their political superiors (Barzelay, 2001). During the last few decades, cutbacks provided the rationale to push managers to raise organizational performance while lowering costs. But to do this effectively, performance assessment tools were needed to supplement resource allocation decisions in government, a notion that is not new and can be traced to performance budgeting.

From an individual performance management perspective, employee evaluation is also a chief activity of management. The selection of an evaluation method depends on the reasons and goals of an organization for evaluating the performance of employees. Within an organizational performance management process, employee appraisal systems are emphasized as crucial personnel management or policy tools that relate the performance goals and achievements of employees to those of the organization and its programs

(Nigro et al., 2007). However, in reality, employee evaluation is one of the most difficult and ambiguous personnel functions.The reason being is that, "the more appraisal systems are made objective, the more evident there is no way to avoid subjectivity" and "although communication of negative information is difficult, not communicating it can be worse"(Berman et al., 2012, pp. 374-375). The focus of performance measurement and management has changed over time in accordance with the dominant understanding of what constitutes 'government performance'. In times of shrinking public budgets and a discourse of the need for less government, as in the 1980s, performance measurement and management tends to focus on inputs and efficiency. At present, the decline in trust of public institutions is pushing performance measurement systems towards measurement of quality of life indicators and the quality of governance. In this respect, performance measurement and management are children of their time, with a new generation emerging about every decade.

1. Organizational Effectiveness Dimensions

- Overall Effectiveness
- Productivity
- Efficiency
- Profit
- Quality
- Accidents
- Growth
- Absenteeism
- Turnover
- Job Satisfaction
- Motivation
- Morale
- Control
- Conflict / Cohesion
- Flexibility / Adaptation

- Planning and Goal Setting
- Goal Consensus
- Internalization of Organizational Goals
- Role and Norm Congruence
- Managerial Interpersonal Skills
- Managerial Task Skills
- Information Management and Communication
- Readiness
- Utilization of Environment
- Evaluations by External Entities
- Stability
- Value of Human Resources
- Participation and Shared Influence
- Training and Development Emphasis
- Achievement Emphasis

Source: Campbell (1977)

2. A Typology of Performance Indicators

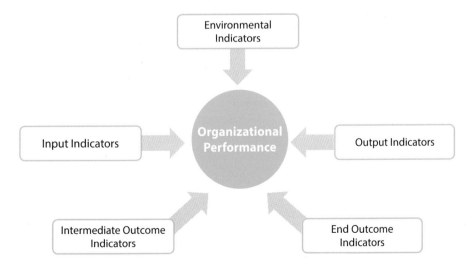

Source: Bovaird & Löffler (2009)

293

① Environmental Indicators

Bovaird & Löffler (2009)

Age structure
Economic indicators such as growth of GDP

② Input Indicators

Bovaird & Löffler (2009)

Number of employees
Money spent
Number of hospital beds
Number of public buses

③ Output Indicators

Bovaird & Löffler (2009)

Number of pupils taught
Number of discharged patients
Vehicle miles

④ Intermediate Outcome Indicators

Bovaird & Löffler (2009)

New knowledge
Increased skills
Number of recovered patients

⑤ End Outcome Indicators

Bovaird & Löffler (2009)

Increased grades achieved in schools
Reductions in unemployment
Increased health and well-being

3. Trends and Development in the Pursuit of Effective Public Management

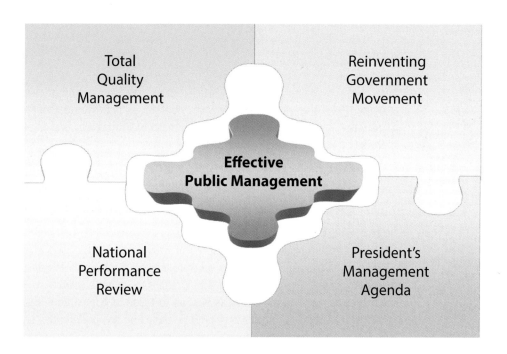

Total Quality Management

Reinventing Government Movement

Effective Public Management

National Performance Review

President's Management Agenda

1) Total Quality Management (TQM)

Rainey (2014, p. 465)

The basic principles of TQM emphasize that successful total quality efforts depend heavily on commitment and strategic implementation.

Rainey (2014, p. 459)

TQM raises challenging alternatives for management.
It has clearly influenced the objectives of current government reform efforts, such as focusing on the customers, the use of teams, and continuous improvement.

Rainey (2014, pp. 459-465)

Deming (1986) emphasized teamwork, continuous improvement of the production system, creating trust and climate of innovation, and eliminating numerical production quotas.

Rainey (2014, p. 464)

Deming (1986) argued that measures of quality should be used at all phases of production and should be the basis for continuous efforts to improve quality. The organization should strive to improve relative to its own previous quality measures as well as to those of comparable organizations. The quality measures should be based on the preferences and point of view of the organization's customers.

Source: Deming (1986), Rainey (2014, pp. 459-465)

2) Reinventing Government Movement (REGO)

Catalytic Government	Customer-Driven Government
Community-Owned Government	Enterprising Government
Competitive Government	Anticipatory Government
Mission-Drive Government	Decentralized Government
Results-Oriented Government	Market-Oriented Government

Reinventing Government Movement

Source: Osborn & Gabler (1992), Rainey (2014, pp. 467-468)

① Catalytic Government

Osborn & Gaebler (1992)

"Leverage" government authority and resource by suing private-and non-profit-sector resources and energies, through such strategies as privatization of public services and public-private partnerships.

Source: Osborn & Gabler (1992), Rainey (2014, pp. 467-468)

Osborn & Gaebler (1992)

Government should "steer" rather that "row", by emphasizing directions and priorities but letting private and nonprofit organizations deliver services and carry out projects.

Source: Osborn & Gabler (1992), Rainey (2014, pp. 467-468)

② Community-Owned Government

Osborn & Gaebler (1992)

Empower local communities and groups. Allow more local control through such strategies as community policing and resident control of public housing.

Source: Osborn & Gabler (1992), Rainey (2014, pp. 467-468)

③ Competitive Government

Osborn & Gaebler (1992)

Introduce more competition between government and private organization, within government, and between private organizations through such strategies as competitive contracting, private competition with public service, and school choice and voucher program.

Source: Osborn & Gabler (1992), Rainey (2014, pp. 467-468)

④ Mission-Drive Government

Osborn & Gaebler (1992)

Focus government programs on their missions rather than on bureaucratic rules and procedures, through such strategies as flexible personnel rules and procedures (such as broader, more flexible pay categories, as studied in the China Lake Experiments).

Source: Osborn & Gabler (1992), Rainey (2014, pp. 467-468)

⑤ Results-Oriented Government

Osborn & Gaebler (1992)

Place more emphasis on outcomes rather than inputs, through greater investment in performance measures, including using them in budgeting and evaluation systems.

Source: Osborn & Gabler (1992), Rainey (2014, pp. 467-468)

⑥ Customer-Driven Government

Give customers of public programs and services more influence over them.
Give customers more choice through voucher systems and competition among service providers.

Source: Osborn & Gabler (1992), Rainey (2014, pp. 467-468)

⑦ Enterprising Government

Find ways to earn money through user fees, profitable sus of government resources and programs, and innovative cost-saving and privatization projects.

Source: Osborn & Gabler (1992), Rainey (2014, pp. 467-468)

⑧ Anticipatory Government

Prevent problems they occur rather than curing them after they do, through strategic planning, futures commissions, long-range budgeting, interdepartmental planning and budgeting, and innovative prevention programs in environmental protection, crime, fire, and other service areas.

Source: Osborn & Gabler (1992), Rainey (2014, pp. 467-468)

⑨ Decentralized Government

Decentralize government activities through such approaches as relaxing rules and hierarchical controls, participatory management innovative management, employee development, and lavor-management partnerships.

Source: Osborn & Gabler (1992), Rainey (2014, pp. 467-468)

⑩ Market-Oriented Government

Osborn & Gaebler (1992)

Use economic market mechanisms to achieve public policy goals and deliver public services, through such techniques as pollution taxes, deposit fees on bottles, user fees, tax credits, and vouchers.

Source: Osborn & Gabler (1992), Rainey (2014, pp. 467-468)

3) National Performance Review (NPR)

Cutting Red Tape
Biennial budgeting
Decentralize personnel policy
Streamline procurement
Eliminate unneeded regulations
Empower state and local governments

National Performance Review

Customer-Driven Influence
Market dynamics

Empowering Employees
Decentralize decisions making
Results orientation
Provide better training

Greater efficiency
Eliminate unnecessary programs
Generate more income
and collect more debt
Utilize existing technologies

Source: Rainey (2014, pp. 469-472)

4) President's Management Agenda

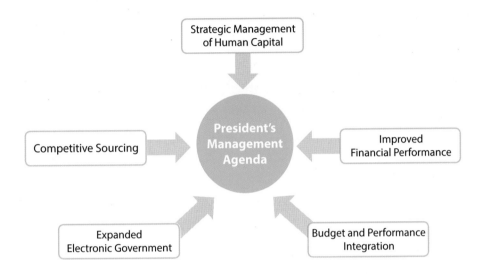

Source: Rainey (2014, pp. 472-473)

4. Characteristics of High Performance Organization

1) Condition

Source: Rainey & Steinbauer (1999), Rainey (2014, pp. 462-463)

2) Effective relations with other stakeholders

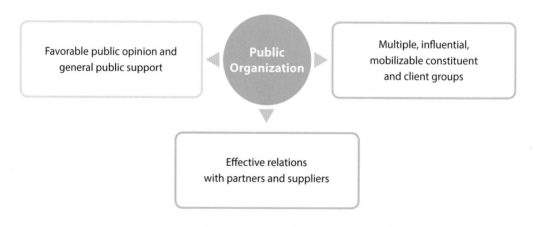

Source: Rainey & Steinbauer (1999), Rainey (2014, pp. 462-463)

3) Responsive autonomy in relation to political oversight and influence

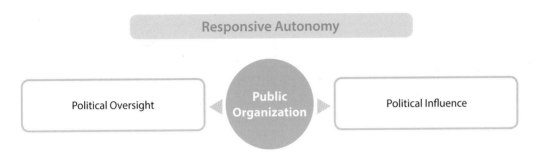

Source: Rainey & Steinbauer (1999), Rainey (2014, pp. 462-463)

4) Mission Valence

Source: Rainey & Steinbauer (1999), Rainey (2014, pp. 462-463)

5) Strong organizational culture, linked to mission

Source: Rainey & Steinbauer (1999), Rainey (2014, pp. 462-463)

303

6) Effective Leadership

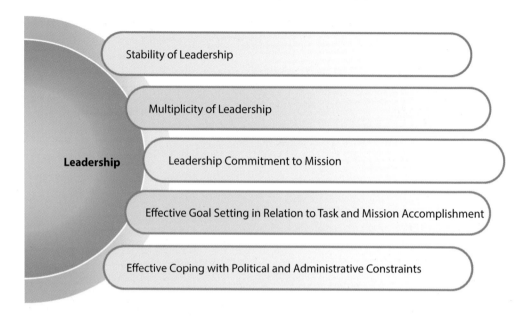

Source: Rainey & Steinbauer (1999), Rainey (2014, pp. 462-463)

7) Effective task design

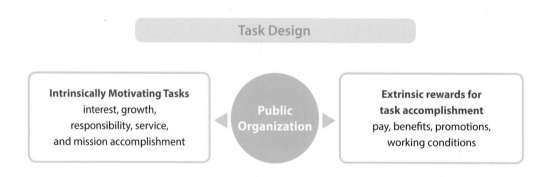

Source: Rainey & Steinbauer (1999), Rainey (2014, pp. 462-463)

8) Effective development of human resource

Human Resource Development

Effective recruitment, selection, placement, training, and development

◀ **Public Organization** ▶

Values and preferences among recruits and members that support task and mission motivation

Source: Rainey & Steinbauer (1999), Rainey (2014, pp. 462-463)

9) High levels of professionalism among members

Professionalism

High levels of special knowledge and skills related to task and mission accomplishment

◀ **Public Organization** ▶

Commitment to task and mission accomplishment

▼

High levels of public service professionalism

Source: Rainey & Steinbauer (1999), Rainey (2014, pp. 462-463)

305

10) High levels of motivation among members

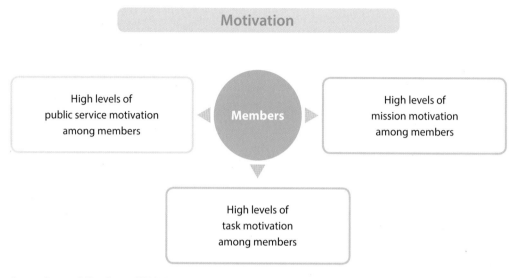

Source: Rainey & Steinbauer (1999), Rainey (2014, pp. 462-463)

5. Performance and Effectiveness Assessment Tools: Focus on U.S. Federal Agencies

1) OMB (Office of Management and Budget) Scorecard

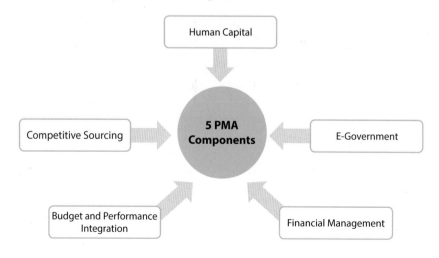

Source: Joaquin & Park (2013, p. 57)

Joaquin & Park (2013, p. 57)

The Scorecard was a traffic-light scoring system that graded 26 agencies quarterly on the 5 PMA components. OMB published the Scorecard throughout the Bush administration, hinting the budgetary sanctions connected to the tool.

Joaquin & Park (2013, p. 57)

OMB and agencies set "Green Plans" and milestones that agencies must strive to meet for each component. All agencies started in red. Yellow indicated progress and green means that agencies have met their goals and targets. Agencies could be downgraded from green to yellow to red again.

2) PART (Performance Assessment Rating Tool) Scores

Program Purpose and Design scores
Reflect whether the program has a clear purpose and if the program is Designed to meet that purpose (20%)

Strategic Planning scores
Reflect whether the program's agency has established suitable annual goals and long-term goals for its programs (10%)

PART score

Program Management scores
Indicate whether the program has good management including appropriate financial oversight controls and program improvement methods (20%)

Program Results scores
Indicate whether the program is achieving performance results according to strategic planning goals (50%)

Source: Joaquin & Park (2013, p. 57)

Joaquin & Park (2013, p. 57)

Approximately 30 questions are required for federal managers to answer about program sections and a set of weights is assigned to each section, resulting in a final cumulative PART score.

Joaquin & Park (2013, p. 57)

PART results were meant to inform budgetary decisions in Congress and OMB.

3) BPTW (Best Places to Work) Index

Joaquin & Park (2013, p. 57)

The BPTW in the Federal Government rankings were designed to improve the public sector work environment and organizational effectiveness.
Partnership for Public Service and American University's ISPPI use data from the Office of Personnel Management's Federal Human Capital Survey to rank 279 federal agencies and subcomponents.

Joaquin & Park (2013, p. 57)

The BPTW score is calculated both for the organization as a whole and also for specific demographic groups.
Agencies and subcomponents are also scored in 10 workplace environment ("best in class") (www.bestplacestowork.org/BPTW/about/).

3 From Theory to Practice

1. Agency Analysis

Ministry of Strategy and Finance

Ministry of Strategy and Finance (MOSF) is control tower of an economic policy in Korea. MOSF is committed to driving strong economic development and developing engines of growth through concerted efforts of its bureaus and offices to ensure stable and sound macroeconomic management, effective policy coordination, efficient allocation of national resources, sound fiscal management, reform of public organizations, a rational and equitable tax system, and strong international economic cooperation. Developing and coordinating economic policies and strategiesto efficiently manage the nation's finances (Retrieved from:http://english.mosf.go.kr).

Main tasks of MOSF are as follows: 1) Planning and establishing mid - to long-term national development strategies; 2) Formulating and coordinating economic and fiscal policies; 3) Planning, executing and managing budgets and public funds and monitoring and reviewing expenditures; 4) Developing and administering policies in regard to taxes, tariffs, the national treasury, government accounting, lottery, and public fund management; 5) Overseeing public organizations, evaluating their performances, and promoting management innovation; 6) Formulating and implementing policies for international finance and foreign exchange and strengthening international financial cooperation; and 7) Promoting economic cooperation with both developing and advanced economies and taking measures to facilitate FTAs in Korea.

Especially, one of the most important tasks of the agency is the conduct of Public Institution Performance Evaluation. This assessment was carried out on the public enterprise and quasi-governmental institution every year.

Public Institution Performance Evaluation was conducted on 30 public enterprises and 86 quasi-governmental institutions in 2013. The 2013 evaluation results are as follows: 1) 2 agencies received grade A; 2) 39 agencies received grade B; 3) 46 agencies received grade B; 4) 19 agencies received grade D; and 5) 11 agencies received grade E. The results of Public Institution Performance Evaluation are reflected in the CEO's term in office and also directly linked to incentive of managers and employees.

Assessment System

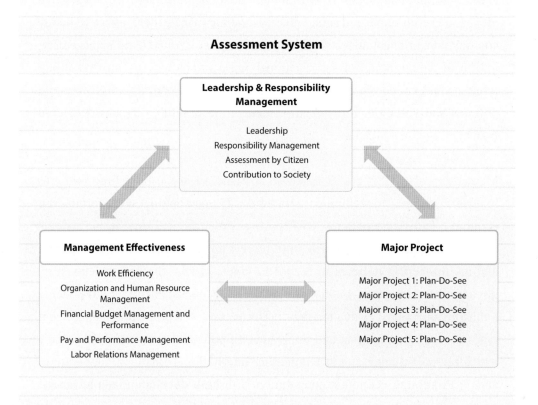

Leadership & Responsibility Management

Leadership
Responsibility Management
Assessment by Citizen
Contribution to Society

Management Effectiveness

Work Efficiency
Organization and Human Resource Management
Financial Budget Management and Performance
Pay and Performance Management
Labor Relations Management

Major Project

Major Project 1: Plan-Do-See
Major Project 2: Plan-Do-See
Major Project 3: Plan-Do-See
Major Project 4: Plan-Do-See
Major Project 5: Plan-Do-See

Discussion Questions on Agency Case

1   What conditions and principles are typically involved in the TQM approach? What studies have sought to assess the implementation of REGO, and what were the main findings? Who were Osborne and Gaebler, and what strategies did they propose for effective government? In what ways has REGO been influential? In what ways has it been controversial?

2   In what ways does Total Quality Management (TQM) differ from the "command and control" approach to management? What effects do you think leadership and motivation might have on the success of TQM efforts? In what ways might the organizational context matter to TQM efforts?

3   Evaluate the following comment by Osborne and Gaebler: "…governments is tall, sluggish, over-centralized, and preoccupied with rules and regulations…We designed public agencies to protect the public against politicians and bureaucrats gaining too much power or misusing public money. In making it difficult to steal the public's money, we made it virtually impossible to manage the public's money….In attempting to control virtually everything, we became so obsessed with dictating how things should be done—regulating the process, controlling the inputs— that we ignored the outcomes, the results….Government can—and must— compete with for-profit businesses, nonprofit agencies, and other units of government."

Class Exercises

1   Take an annual report from a public agency with which you are familiar. Identify the performance indicators reported in it and classify them according to the 10 elements of MAF. Do you think that the balance between these types of performance indicator is appropriate for this agency?

2   Take one of the performance indicators identified in the theory synopsis. Consider how an individual, a unit or a whole organization might find ways of influencing the reported level of that indicator in order to make their work look more successful. Foreach of these possible abuses, suggest ways in which that kind of behavior could bemade less easy or less likely to succeed.

3   Interview the head of a public agency or government department about the goals of his/her organization. Record the interviewee's responses to the three open-ended questions below. Relying on the literature reviewed in this chapter on organizational performance and effectiveness, write a report describing what you have learned. Are the responses consistent with comments in the chapter and with the cited literature on the topic?

   - In what ways and to what degree do the agency's stated goals influence organizational effectiveness?
   - How is effectiveness measured?
   - What difficulties have you encountered in assessing your agency's performance or effectiveness?

2. Research Notes

Exploring the Topography of Performance and Effectiveness of U.S. Federal Agencies

We have a proliferation of tools to evaluate federal agencies' performance and effectiveness. This article explores how effectiveness and performance values are distributed across government agencies based on three well-known assessment instruments used during the Bush administration: the Office of Management and Budget (OMB) Management Scorecard, the Performance Assessment Rating Tool (PART), and the Best Places to Work (BPTW) survey. A cluster analysis of the scores from these assessment tools allows us to examine the topography of the agencies in terms of the relationship between the tools and the context of performance, namely, the type of mission carried out by the agencies. Depending on the policy mission type, some agencies fare better in some assessment measures than others. By comparing scores from PART and OMB Scorecard with the BPTW survey, we also find a complex picture when leadership-driven performance metrics are compared with the results of an employee-based assessment of organizational effectiveness.

Research Framework

Factors within Clusters	Cluster 1: High HR & Fin Mgt Agencies	Cluster 2: High Contracng (A-76) & E-gov Agencies	Cluster 3: High PART Agencies
• Human Capital • Competitive Sourcing • Financial Performance • E-Government • Budget & Performance Integraon • PART (Effecve)	Commerce Energy Labor EPA GSA OPM SSA	Education HHS Justice Interior NASA	DOD State Treasury Smithsonian
	N = 7	N = 5	N = 4

Factors within Clusters	Cluster 1: Performance Mgt-Oriented Agencies	Cluster 2: WLB-Oriented Agencies	Cluster 3: Team & Leadership-Oriented Agencies
• Strategic Management • Teamwork • Leadership • Performance Culture • Training & Development • Work life-Balance Management • Diversity Management	Commerce EPA State NASA NSF OMB	Army Corps DOD Education Energy HHS Justice Treasury SSA	Justice GSA Labor Treasury USAID Energy
	N = 6	N = 8	N = 6

Source: Joaquin & Park (2013)

Research Note 2

Determinants of Job Satisfaction and Turnover Intentions of Public Employees : Evidence from U.S. Federal Agencies

The purpose of this study is to probe the main determinants of job satisfaction (JS) and turnover intention (TI) in the public sector, as identified in the relevant literature: goal congruence, intrinsic and extrinsic work motivation, and interpersonal trust. Drawing on Simon's two-factor theory, as well as employing a systematic conceptual and empirical model, this research analyzes two dimensions of TI among public employees (conflictual TI and developmental TI) to identify important antecedents and mediating conditions (pull factors and push factors) of TI. Large data sets from the Merit Principles Survey (MPS) are used to develop an "antecedent-mediator-outcome" model that empirically analyzes and tests the direct and indirect effects of a set of attitudinal and behavioral influences on JS and two types of TI within U.S. federal agencies. The research finds that certain predictors and mediators play major roles in meaningfully diminishing the levels of conflictual TI and developmental TI while significantly boosting JS. Based on a discussion of the main findings, research and practical implications for public management theory and practice are provided.

Research Framework

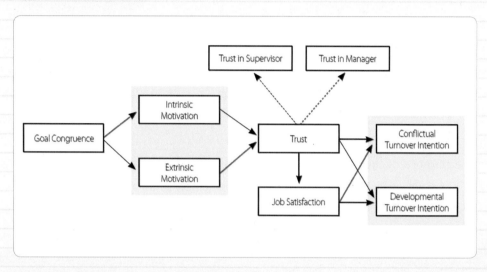

Source: Kim & Park (2014)

Appendix 1

1. Government Office

1) The Central Government

(1) The Executive Branch

- The Blue House - http://www.president.go.kr
- Prime Minister's Office - http://www.pmo.go.kr
- National Intelligence Service(NIS) - http://www.nis.go.kr
- The Board of Audit and Inspection of Korea(BAI) - http://www.bai.go.kr
- Ministry of Strategy and Finance(MOSF) - http://www.mosf.go.kr
- Ministry of Science, ICT & Future Planning(MSIP) - http://www.msip.go.kr
- Ministry of Education(MOE) - http://www.mest.go.kr
- Ministry of Foreign Affairs(MOFA) - http://www.mofat.go.kr
- Ministry of Unification(MOU) - http://www.unikorea.go.kr
- Ministry of Justice(MOJ) - http://www.moj.go.kr
- Ministry of National Defense(MND) - http://www.mnd.go.kr
- Ministry of Security and Public Administration(MOSPA) - http://www.mopas.go.kr
- Ministry of Culture, Sports and Tourism(MCST) - http://www.mcst.go.kr
- Ministry of Agriculture, Food and Rural Affairs(MAFRA) - http://www.mafra.go.kr/
- Ministry of Trade, Industry & Energy(MOTIE) - http://www.mke.go.kr
- Ministry of Health & Welfare(MW) - http://www.mw.go.kr
- Ministry of Environment(MEV) - http://www.me.go.kr
- Ministry of Employment and Labor(MOEL) - http://www.moel.go.kr
- Ministry of Gender Equality & Family(MOGEF) - http://www.mogef.go.kr
- Ministry of Land, Infrastructure and Transport(MOLIT) - http://www.mltm.go.kr
- Ministry of Oceans and Fisheries - http://www.mof.go.kr

- Ministry of Government Legislation(MOLEG) - http://www.moleg.go.kr
- Ministry of Patriots and Veterans Affairs(MPVA) - http://www.mpva.go.kr
- Ministry of Food and Drug Safety(MFDS) - http://www.mfds.go.kr
- National Tax Service(NTS) - http://www.nts.go.kr
- Korea Customs Service(KCS) - http://www.customs.go.kr
- Public Procurement Service(PPS) - http://www.pps.go.kr
- Statistics Korea - http://www.kostat.go.kr
- Supreme Prosecutors' Office(SPO) - http://www.spo.go.kr
- Military Manpower Administration(MMA) - http://www.mma.go.kr
- Defense Acquisition Program Administration(DAPA) - http://www.dapa.go.kr
- Korean National Police Agency(KNPA) - http://www.police.go.kr
- National Emergency Management Agency(NEMA) - http://www.nema.go.kr
- Cultural Heritage Administration(CHA) - http://www.cha.go.kr
- Rural Development Administration(RDA) - http://www.rda.go.kr
- Korea Forest Service(KFS) - http://www.forest.go.kr
- Small and Medium Business Administration(SMBA) - http://www.smba.go.kr
- Korean Intellectual Property Office(KIPO) - http://www.kipo.go.kr
- Korea Meteorological Administration(KMA) - http://www.kma.go.kr
- Multifunctional Administrative City Construction Agency(MACCA) - http://www.macc.go.kr
- Korea Coast Guard(KCG) - http://www.kcg.go.kr
- Korea Communications Commission(KCC) - http://www.kcc.go.kr
- National Human Rights Commission of Korea(NHRCK) - http://www.humanrights.go.kr
- Korea Fair Trade Commission(KFTC) - http://www.ftc.go.kr
- Financial Services Commission(FSC) - http://www.fsc.go.kr
- Anti-Corruption & Civil Rights Commission(ACRC) - http://www.acrc.go.kr
- Nuclear Safety and Security Commission(NSSC) http://www.nssc.go.kr

(2) The Legislative Branch

- The National Assembly of the Republic of Korea - http://www.assembly.go.kr
- Committee

: House Steering Committee - http://steering.na.go.kr

: Legislation & Judiciary Committee - http://legislation.na.go.kr

: National Policy Committee - http://policy.na.go.kr

: Strategy & Finance Committee - http://finance.na.go.kr

: Science, ICT, Future Planning, Broadcasting & Communications Committee -
  http://future.na.go.kr

: Education, Culture, Sports & Tourism Committee - http://educulture.na.go.kr

: Foreign Affairs & Unification Committee - http://uft.na.go.kr

: National Defense Committee - http://defense.na.go.kr

: Security & Public Administration Committee - http://adminhom.na.go.kr

: Agriculture, Food, Rural Affairs, Oceans & Fisheries - http://agri.na.go.kr

: Trade, Industry and Energy Committee - http://industry.na.go.kr

: Health & Welfare Committee - http://health.na.go.kr

: Environment & Labor Committee - http://environment.na.go.kr

: Land Infrastructure and Transport Committee - http://ltc.na.go.kr

: Intelligence Committee - http://intelligence.na.go.kr

: Gender Equality and Family Committee - http://women.na.go.kr

: Special Committee on Budget & Accounts - http://budget.na.go.kr

: Special Committee on Ethics - http://moral.na.go.kr/servlet/Controller?

• National Assembly Secretariat - http://nas.na.go.kr

• National Assembly Budget Office - http://www.nabo.go.kr

• National Assembly Research Service - http://www.nars.go.kr

• National Assembly Library - http://www.nanet.go.kr/main.jsp

• National Assembly Visitor Center - http://memorial.na.go.kr

• National Assembly Television - http://www.natv.go.kr

(3) The Judicial Branch

• Supreme Court of Korea - http://www.scourt.go.kr

• High Court Armed Forces - http://www.hcaf.mil.kr

• Patent Court of Korea - http://patent.scourt.go.kr

• Seoul Central District Court - http://seoul.scourt.go.kr

• Seoul High Court - http://slgodung.scourt.go.kr

• Seoul Administrative Court - http://sladmin.scourt.go.kr

• Seoul Family Court - http://slfamily.scourt.go.kr

• Judicial Research & Training Institute - http://jrti.scourt.go.kr

• Sentencing Commission - http://sc.scourt.go.kr

• Constitutional Court of Korea - http://www.ccourt.go.kr

2) The Local Government

• Seoul Metropolitan Government - http://www.seoul.go.kr

• Busan Metropolitan City - http://www.busan.go.kr

• Daegu Metropolitan City - http://www.daegu.go.kr

• Incheon Metropolitan City - http://www.inchcon.go.kr

• Gwanju Metropolitan City - http://www.gwangju.go.kr

• Daejeon Metropolitan City - http://www.daejeon.go.kr

• Ulsan Metropolitan City - http://www.ulsan.go.kr

• Gyeonggi Province - http://www.gg.go.kr

• Gangwon Province - http://www.provin.gangwon.kr

• Chungcheongbuk-Do Province - http://www.cb21.net

• Chungcheognam-Do Province - http://www.chungnam.net

• Jeollabuk-Do Province - http://www.jeonbuk.go.kr

• Jeolanam-Do Province - http://www.jeonnam.go.kr

• Gyeongsangbuk-Do Province - http://www.gyeongbuk.go.kr

• Gyeongsangnam-Do Province - http://www.gsnd.net

• Jeju Special Self-Governing Province - http://www.jeju.go.kr

• Sejong Special Self-Governing City - http://www.sejong.go.kr

2. Public Institution

1) Public Enterprise / Government-owned Corporation

(1) Market-oriented Public Enterprise

- Korea Gas Corporation - http://www.kogas.or.kr
- Korea National Oil Corporation - http://www.knoc.co.kr
- Korea Electric Power Corporation - http://www.kepco.co.kr
- Korea District Heating Corporation - http://www.kdhc.co.kr
- Korea Hydro & Nuclear Power Company Limited - http://www.khnp.co.kr
- Korea Midland Power Company Limited - http://www.komipo.co.kr
- Korea Western Power Company Limited - http://www.iwest.co.kr
- Korea East-West Power Company Limited - http://www.ewp.co.kr
- Korea Southern Power Company Limited - http://www.kospo.co.kr
- Korea South East Power Company Limited - http://www.kosep.co.kr
- Incheon International Airport Corporation - http://www.airport.kr
- Korea Airports Corporation - http://www.airport.co.kr
- Busan Port Authority - http://www.busanpa.com
- Incheon Port Authority - http://www.icpa.or.kr

(2) Quasi Market-oriented Public Enterprise

- Korea Minting, Security Printing & ID Card Operation Corporation
  - http://www.komsco.com
- Korea Tourism Organization - http://kto.visitkorea.or.kr
- Korea Racing Authority - http://www.kra.co.kr
- Korea Resources Corporation - http://www.kores.or.kr
- Korea Coal Corporation - http://www.kocoal.or.kr
- Korea Housing Guarantee Company Limited - http://www.khgc.co.kr
- Jeju Free International City Development Center - http://www.jdcenter.com

- Korea Appraisal Board - http://www.kab.co.kr

- Korea Expressway Corporation - http://www.ex.co.kr

- Korea Water Resources Corporation - http://www.kwater.or.kr

- Korea Land & Housing Corporation - http://www.lh.or.kr

- Korea Railroad Corporation - http://www.korail.com

- Yeosu Gwangyang Port Authority - http://www.ygpa.or.kr

- Ulsan Port Authority - http://www.upa.or.kr

- Korea Marine Environment Management Corporation - http://www.koem.or.kr

- Korea Broadcast Advertising Corporation - http://www.kobaco.co.kr

2) Quasi Non-Governmental organization

(1) Type I

- Korea Teachers' Pension - http://www.tp.or.kr

- Government Employees Pension Service - http://www.geps.or.kr

- Korean Film Council - http://www.kofic.or.kr

- Korea Sports Promotion Foundation - http://www.kspo.or.kr

- Art Council Korea - http://www.arko.or.kr

- Korea Press Foundation - http://www.kpf.or.kr

- Korea Trade Insurance Corporation - http://www.ksure.or.kr

- Korea Radioactive Waste Management Corporation - http://www.krmc.or.kr

- National Pension Service - http://www.nps.or.kr

- Korea Workers' Compensation & Welfare Service - http://www.kcomwel.or.kr

- Korea Asset Management Corporation - http://www.kamco.or.kr

- Korea Technology Finance Corporation - http://www.kibo.or.kr

- Korea Credit Guarantee Fund - http://www.kodit.co.kr

- Korea Deposit Insurance Corporation - http://www.kdic.or.kr

- Korea Housing-Finance Corporation - http://www.hf.go.kr

- Korea Communications Agency - http://www.kca.kr

- Small & Medium Business Corporation - http://www.sbc.or.kr

(2) Type Ⅱ

- Korea Education and Research Information Service - http://www.keris.or.kr
- Korea Foundation for the Advancement of Science & Creativity - http://www.kofac.re.kr
- National Research Foundation of Korea - http://www.nrf.re.kr
- Korea Student Aid Foundation - http://www.kosaf.go.kr
- Korea Elevator Safety Institute - http://www.kesi.or.kr
- National Information Society Agency - http://www.nia.or.kr
- The Korea International Broadcasting Foundation - http://www.arirang.co.kr
- Korea Creative Content Agency - http://www.dccenter.kr
- Korea Agro-Fisheries & Food Trade Corporation - http://www.at.or.kr
- Korea Institute for Animal Products Quality Evaluation - http://www.ekape.or.kr
- Korea Rural Community Corporation - http://www.ekr.or.kr
- Korea Fisheries Resources Agency - http://www.fira.or.kr
- Korea Livestock Products HACCP Accreditation Service - http://www.ihaccp.or.kr
- Korea Institute of Planning & Evaluation for Technology in Food, Agriculture, Forestry & Fisheries - http://www.ipet.re.kr
- Korea Agency of Education, Promotion & Information Service in Food, Agriculture, Forestry & Fisheries - http://www.epis.or.kr
- Korea Petroleum Quality & Distribution Authority - http://www.kpetro.or.kr
- Korea Trade-Investment Promotion Agency - http://www.kotra.or.kr
- Korea Energy Management Corporation - http://www.kemco.or.kr
- Korea Institute of Ceramic Engineering and Technology - http://www.kicet.re.kr
- Korea Postal Logistics Agency - http://www.pola.or.kr
- Postal Savings & Insurance Development Institute - http://www.posid.or.kr
- Korea Gas Safety Corporation - http://www.kgs.or.kr
- Mine Reclamation Corporation - http://www.mireco.or.kr
- Korea Institute of Design Promotion - http://www.kidp.or.kr
- Korea Testing Laboratory - http://www.ktl.re.kr
- Korea Institute for Advancement of Technology - http://www.kiat.or.kr
- Korea Evaluation Institute of Industrial Technology - http://www.keit.re.kr

- Korea Industrial Complex Corporation - http://www.kicox.or.kr
- Korea Institute of Energy Technology Evaluation and Planning - http://www.ketep.re.kr
- Korea Postal Service Agency - http://www.posa.or.kr
- Korea Electrical Safety Corporation - http://www.kesco.or.kr
- Korea Power Exchange - http://www.kpx.or.kr
- National IT Industry Promotion Agency - http://www.nipa.kr
- Health Insurance Review & Assessment Service - http://www.hira.or.kr
- National Health Insurance Service - http://www.nhic.or.kr
- Korea Health Industry Development Institute - http://www.khidi.or.kr
- Korea Labor Force Development Institute for the Aged - http://www.kordi.go.kr
- Korea Health and Welfare Information Service - http://www.khwis.or.kr
- Korea Human Resource Development Institute for Health & Welfare
- http://www.kohi.or.kr
- Korea National Park Service - http://www.knps.or.kr
- Korea Environment Corporation - http://www.keco.or.kr
- Korea Environmental Industry & Technology Institute - http://www.keiti.re.kr
- Korea Employment Information Service - http://www.keis.or.kr
- Korea Occupational Safety and Health Agency - http://www.kosha.or.kr
- Human Resources Development Service of Korea - http://www.hrdkorea.or.kr
- Korea Employment Agency for the Disabled - http://www.kead.or.kr
- Korea Elevator Safety Technology Institute - http://www.kest.or.kr
- Korea Youth Counseling & Welfare Institute - http://www.kyci.or.kr
- Korea Youth Work Agency - http://www.kywa.or.kr
- Korea Transportation Safety Authority - http://www.ts2020.kr
- Korea Agency for Infrastructure Technology Advancement - http://www.kaia.re.kr
- Korea Infrastructure Safety & Technology Corporation - http://www.kistec.or.kr
- Korea Rail Network Authority - http://www.kr.or.kr
- Korea Cadastral Survey Corporation - http://www.kcsc.or.kr
- Korea Ship Safety Technology Authority - http://www.kst.or.kr
- Korea Institute of Maritime and Fisheries Technology - http://www.seaman.or.kr
- Korea Consumer Agency - http://www.kca.go.kr

- Korea Securities Depository - http://www.ksd.or.kr

- Korea Exchange - http://www.krx.co.kr

- Korea Internet & Security Agency - http://www.kisa.or.kr

- Korea Institute of Nuclear Safety - http://www.kins.re.kr

- The Independence Hall of Korea - http://www.i815.or.kr

- Korea Veterans Health Service - http://www.bohun.or.kr

- Korea Forestry Promotion Institute - http://www.kofpi.or.kr

- Road Traffic Authority - http://www.koroad.or.kr/

- Korea Fire Institute of Industry & Technology - http://www.kfi.or.kr

- Foundation of Agricultural Technology Commercialization & Transfer

- http://www.fact.or.kr

- Korea Technology & Information Promotion Agency for SMEs - http://www.tipa.or.kr

- Small Enterprise Development Agency - http://www.seda.or.kr

- Korea Meteorological Industry Promotion Agency - http://www.kmipa.or.kr/

Appendix 2

Dear Members,

The School of Public Affairs and Administration (SPAA) at Rutgers--Newark is looking for case studies to advance the classroom learning experience of students pursuing public and nonprofit management studies. We are especially interested in case studies that address contemporary topics in the public and nonprofit sectors with real-time practical applications.

Proposals of interest could address one of the following topics:

- Public/Nonprofit Administration
- Organizational Theory
- Human Resources and Diversity
- Decision Making
- Politics/Policy Making
- Multi-Level Governance/Networking
- Performance Measurement and Management
- Program Evaluation
- Budgeting and Finance
- Leadership
- Ethics
- Technology
- Community Service/Citizen Participation
- Future Opportunities and Issues

Case studies may be based on real-world events or fictionalized situations, if relevant to one of the suggested topics. Most importantly, articles must bring application to the field of study and key questions that lead to classroom discussions. It is preferred that case studies be linked to multi-media sources – news, videos, movies, social networks, and others.

A proposal should be double spaced, one page, and using 12-point font size. Following items should be included in each proposal:

1. Summary of a single or multiple case study, linked to real-time and place-based public or nonprofit organizational issues (no more than 250 words)
2. Discussion of primary topics/issues/problems
3. Application of the case study to classroom learning and teaching
4. Multimedia links that support the case study
5. Author(s)' name, title, affiliation, and contact information

We encourage academics, practitioners, and doctoral students to submit a case study proposal to speng@rutgers.edu. Any questions regarding the proposal submission process can be directed to: Shuyang Peng, Research assistant at speng@rutgers.edu (The subject line should read, "Submission of Case Proposal"). Please visit the link below to learn more about the cases and simulation portal.

Source: http://casesimportal.newark.rutgers.edu/

References

Adams, J. S. (1963), Toward an understanding inequity. *Journal of Abnormal and Social Psychology, 67,* 422-436.

Aldrich, H. E. (1979). *Organizational evolving.* Sage.

Allison, G. T. Jr. (1983). Public and private management: Are they fundamentally alike in all unimportant respects?. In L. Perry & K. L. Kraemer (Eds.), *Public management: Public and private perspectives* (pp.72-92). Mayfield.

Baek, W. G. (1993). *Administrative culture in Korea.* Korea University Press.

Barzelay, M. (2001). *The new public management: improving research and policy dialogue.* University of California Press.

Bass, B. M. (1997). Does the transactional-transformational leadership paradigm transcend organizational and national boundaries?. *American Psychologist, 52* (2), 130-139.

Behn, R. (1995). The bog questions of public management. *Public Administration Review, 55*(4), 313-324.

Benn, S. L., & Gaus. G. F (Eds.). (1983). *Public and private in social life.* Taylor-Francis.

Berman, E. M., Bowman, J. S., West, J. P., & Van Wart, M. R. (2012). *Human resource management in public service: Paradoxes, processes, and problems.* Sage Publications.

Berry, F. S. (2007). Strategic planning as a tool for managing organizational change. *International Journal of Public Administration, 30,* 331-346.

Blake, R. R., & McCanse, A. A. (1991). *Leadership dilemmas: Grid solutions.* Gulf Publishing Company.

Blase, P. R., & Mouton, J. S. (1984). Overcoming group welfare. *Harvard Business Review, 62,* 98-108.

Bovaird, T., & Löffler, E. (2009). Public management and governance (2nd ed.). Routledge.

Bozeman, B. (1987). *All organizations are public: Bridging public and private organizational theories.* Jossey-Bass.

Bozeman, B. (2007). *Public values and public interest: Counterbalancing economic individualism.* Georgetown University Press.

Brewer, G. A., & Walker, R. M. (2013). Personnel constraints in public organizations: The impact of reward and punishment on organizational performance. *Public Administration Re-*

view, *73*(1), 121-131.

Brown, M. E., & Treviño, L. K. (2002). Conceptualizing and measuring ethical leadership: Development of an instrument. In *Academy of Management Proceedings* (Vol.2002, No.1, pp.D1~D6). Academy of Management.

Burns, T., & Stalker, G. M. (1961). *The management of innovation*. Tavistock.

Cameron, K. S., Quinn. R. E., J. Degraff., & Thakor, A. V. (2007). *Competing values leadership: Creating value in organization*s. Edward Elgar Publishing.

Campbell, J. P. (1977). On the nature of organizational effectiveness. In P. S. Goodman & J. M. Pennings (Eds), *New perspectives on organizational effectiveness* (pp. 13-55). Jossey-Bass.

Cho, S. J. (1984). *Public administration in Korea*. Parkyoungsa.

Clark, P. B., & Wilson, J. Q. (1961). Incentive systems: A theory of organizations. *Administrative Science Quarterly*, *6*, 129-166.

Cochran, C. E. (1977). Authority and community. *American Political Science Review*, *71*, 546-558.

Coleman, J. S. (1990). *Foundations of social theory*. Harvard University Press.

Crossan, M. L., Lane, H., White, R., & Djurfeldt, L. (1995). Organizational learning: dimensions for a theory. *The International Journal of Organizational Analysis*, *3*(4), 337-360.

Dahl, R. A., & Lindblom, C. E. (1953). *Politics, economics, and welfare*. Harper and Row.

Deal, T. E., & Kennedy, A. A. (1982). Corporate cultures: The rites and rituals of organizational life. Addison-Wesley, 98-103.

Deming, W. E. (1986). *Out of crisis*. MIT Center for Advanced Engineering Study.

Denhardt, R. B., Denhardt, J. V., & Aristigueta, M. P. (2013). *Managing human behavior in public and nonprofit organizations*. Sage.

Denison, D. R., & Spreitzer, G. M. (1991). Organizational culture and organizational development: a competing values approach. *Research in Organizational Change and Development*, *5*, 1-21.

Desimone, R. L., & Werner, J. M. (2012). *Human resource development* (6th ed., International ed.). South-Western Cengage Learning.

Dess, G. G., & Beard, D. W. (1984). Dimensions of organizational task environment. *Administrative Science Quarterly*, *29*, 52-73.

Dewey, J. (1927). *The public and its problems*. Henry Holt.

Downs, A. (1967). Inside bureaucracy. Little, Brown.

Fiedler, F. E. (1964). A contingency model of leadership effectiveness. In L. Berkowitz (Ed.),

Advances in experimental social psychology (pp.149-190). Academinc Press.

Fiedler, F. E. (1967). *A theory of leadership effectiveness*. McGraw-Hill.

Fiedler, F. E., Chemers, M. M., & Mahar, L. (1977). *Improving leadership effectiveness: the leader match concept*. Wiley.

Flanders, L. R., & Utterback, D. (1985). A management excellence inventory: A tool for management development. *Public Administration Review, 45*, 403-410.

Friedrich, C. (1963). *Man and his government*. McGraw-Hill.

Galbraith, J. R. (1997). *Organizational design*, Addison-Wesley.

Galbraith, J. R. (2002). *Designing organizations*. Jossey-Bass.

George, J. M., & Jones, G. R. (1997). Organizational spontaneity in context. *Human Performance, 10*, 153-170.

Gibb, S. (2011). *Human resource development* (3rd ed.). Palgrave Macmillan.

Grant, A. M. (2008). Employees without a cause: The motivational effects of prosocial impact in public service. *International Public Management Journal, 11*(1), 48-66.

Greenleaf, R. K. (2008). *The servant as leader*. RKG Center

Gulick, L. (1937). Notes on the theory of organizations with special reference to government in the United States. In L Gulick, L Urwick (Eds.), *Papers on the science of administration*. Institute of Public Administration.

Hackman, J. R., & Oldham, G. R. (1980). *Work redesign*. Addison-Wesley.

Hallahan, K. (2000). Enhancing motivation, ability, and opportunity to process public relations messages. *Public Relations Review, 26*(4), 463–480.

Hede, A. (2007). Toward an explanation of interpersonal conflict in work group. *Journal of Managerial Psychology, 22*, 25-39.

Herzberg, F. (1968). One more time: How do you motivate employees?. *Havard Business Review, 46*, 36-44.

Herzberg, F., Mausner, B., & Snyderman, B. (1959). *The motivation to work*. John Wiley & Sons.

Hofstede, G. (1980). *Culture's consequences*. Sage.

Hofstede, G., Neuijen, B., Ohayv, D. D., & Sander, G. (1990). Measuring organizational cultures: A qualitative and quantitative study across twenty cases. *Administrative Science Quarterly, 35*, 286-316.

House, R. J., Hanges, P. J., Javidan, M., Dorfman, P. W., & Gupta, V. (Eds.). (2004). *Culture, leadership and organizations: The Globe study of 62 societies*. Sage.

Joaquin, M. E., & Park, S. M. (2013). Exploring the topography of performance and effectiveness of U.S. federal agencies. *Public Personnel Management, 42*(1), 55-74.

Kelly, G., Mulgan, G., & Muers, S. (2002). *Creating public value: An analytical framework
for public service reform*. Discussion paper prepared by the Cabinet Office Strategy Unit,
United Kingdom.

Kim, S., & Park, S. M. (2014). Determinants of job satisfaction and turnover intentions of public employees: Evidence from US federal agencies. *International Review of Public Administration, 19*(1), 63-90.

Kotter, J. P. (1990). *A force for change*. The Free Press.

Kurland, N. B., & Egan, T. D. (1999). Public vs. private perceptions of formalization, outcomes,
and justice. *Journal of Public Administration Research and Theory, 9*, 437-458.

Lawler, E. E., III. (1971), *Pay and organizational effectiveness*. McGraw-Hill.

Lawrence, P. R., & Lorsch, J. W. (1967). *Organization and environment*. Harvard University
Press.

Locke, E. A., & Latham, G. P. (1990). *A theory of goal setting and task performance*. Prentice
Hall.

Locke, E. A., & Latham, G. P. (2002). Building a practically useful theory of goal setting and
task motivation: A 35-year odyssey. *American Psychologist, 57*(9), 705-717.

Maslow, A. (1954). *Motivational and personality*. Harper & Row.

McGregor, D. (1960). *The human side of enterprise*. McGraw-Hill.

McLean, G. N., & McLean, L. D. (2001). If we can't define HRD in one country, how can we
define it in an international context?. *Human Resource Development International, 4*(3),
313-326.

Meinhardt, T., & J. Metelmann. (2009). Pushing the envelope: Creating public value in the labor
market: An empirical study on the role of middle managers. *International Journal of Public Administration, 32*(3-4), 274-312.

Merelman, R. M. (1966). Learning and legitimacy. *American Political Science Review, 60*, 548-
567.

Mintzberg, H. (1979). *The structuring of organizations*. Prentice Hall.

Moore, M. (1995). *Creating public value: Strategic management in government*. Harvard University Press.

Mosher, F. C. (1968). *Democracy and the public service*. Oxford University Press.

Nigro, L. G., Nigro, F. A., & Kellough, J. E. (2007). *The new public personnel administration*.

Wadsworth.

Northouse, P. G. (2004). *Leadership: Theory and practice* (3rd ed.). Sage Publications.

O'Flynn, J. (2007). From new public management to public value: Paradigmatic change and managerial implications. *Australian Journal of Public Administration, 66* (3), 353-366.

Osborn, D., & Gaebler, T. (1992). *Reinventing government.* Addison-Wesley.

Park, C., & Joo, J. (2010). Control over the Korean bureaucracy: A review of the NPM civil service reforms under the Roh Moo-Hyun Government. *Review of Public Personnel Administration, 30*(2), 189–210.

Park, S. M. (2010). The effects of personnel reform systems on Georgia state Employees' attitudes. *Public Management Review, 12*(3), 403-437.

Park, S. M. (2012). Toward the trusted public organization: Untangling the leadership, motivation, and trust relationship in U.S. federal agencies. *The American Review of Public Administration, 42*(5), 562-590.

Park, S. M. (2013). *Public management: A research handbook.* Deayoung Moonhwasa Publishing Company.

Park, S. M., & Ahn, B. I. (2013). Exploring the antecedents and consequences of the acceptance of performance appraisal systems. In S. M. Park (Ed.), *Public management: A research Handbook* (pp. 490-524). Daeyong Moonhwasa Publising Company.

Park, S. M., & Joaquin, M. E. (2012). Of alternating waves and shifting shores: The configuration of reform values in the US federal bureaucracy. *International Review of Administrative Sciences, 78*(3), 514-536.

Park, S. M., & Kim, M. Y. (2013). Research on accountability in the Korean central government agencies: Exploring antecedent and moderating effects of public service motivation, goal clarity, and person-organization fit. In S. M. Park (Ed.), *Public management: A research Handbook* (pp. 338-367). Daeyong Moonhwasa Publising Company.

Park, S. M., & Kim, S. (2013). Performance management in Canadian public agencies: The federal case. In D. S. Kong (Ed.), *Performance Management* (pp. 79-108). Daeyong Moonhwasa Publising Company.

Park, S. M., & Rainey, H. G. (2007). Antecedents, mediators, and consequences of affective, normative, and continuance commitment: Empirical tests of commitment effects in federal agencies. *Review of Public Personnel Administration, 27*(3), 197-226.

Park, S. M., & Rainey, H. G. (2008). Leadership and public service motivation in U.S. federal Agencies. *International Public Management Journal, 11*(1), 109-142.

Park, S. M., & Rainey, H. G. (2012). Work motivation and social communication among public managers. *The International Journal of Human Resource Management, 23*(13), 2630-2660.

Park, S. M., & Word, J. (2012). Driven to service: Intrinsic and extrinsic motivation for public and nonprofit managers. *Public Personnel Management, 41*(4), 681-710.

Park, S. M., & Word, J. (2012). Serving the mission: Organizational antecedents and social consequences of job choice motivation in the nonprofit sector. *International Review of Public Administration, 17*(3), 161-198.

Park, S. M., Miao, Q., & Kim, M. Y. (2013). The roles of integrative leadership for enhancing organizational effectiveness in the Chinese public sector. In S. M. Park (Ed.), *Public management: A research Handbook* (pp. 278-296). Daeyong Moonhwasa Publising Company.

Park, S. M., Park, H. J., & Ryu, E. Y. (2013). Determinants of positive job attitude and behaviour in the Asian work context: Evidence from Korean central government agencies. *Public Management Review, 15*(8), 1154-1184.

Peabody, R. L., & Rourke, F. E. (1965). Public bureaucracies. In J. G. March (Ed.), *Handbook of organizations* (pp. 802-837). Rand McNally.

Perry, J. L, & Rainey, H. G. (1988). The public-private distinction in organization theory: A critique and research strategy. *Academy of Management Review, 13*(2), 182-201.

Perry, J. L., & Porter, L. W. (1982). Factors affecting the context for motivation in public organizations. *Academy of Management Review, 7*, 89-98.

Perry, J. L., & Wise, L. R. (1990). The motivational bases of public service. *Public Administration Review, 50*, 367-373.

Petter, J., Byrnes, P., Choi, D.-L., Fegan, F., & Miller, R. (2002). Dimensions and patterns in employee empowerment: assessing what matters to street-level bureaucrats. *Journal of Public Administration Research and Theory, 12*(3), 377-400.

Pugh, D. S., Hickson, D. J., & Hinings, C. R. (1969). An empirical study taxonomy of work organizations. *Administrative Science Quarterly, 14*, 115-126.

Quinn, R. E., & Kimberly, J. R. (1984). Paradox, planning, and perseverance: Guidelines for managerial practice. In J. R. Kimberly, & R. E. Quiin (Eds.), *Managing organizational transitions*. McGraw-Hill.

Rainey, H. G. & Steinbauer, P. (1999). Galloping elephants: Developing elements of a theory of effective government organizations. *Journal of Public Administration Research and Theory, 9*(1), 1-32.

Rainey, H. G. (1979). Perceptions of incentives in business and government: Implications for civil service reform. *Public Administration Review, 39*(5), 440-448.

Rainey, H. G. (1989). Public management recent research on the political context and managerial roles, structures, and behaviors. *Journal of Management, 152,* 229-50.

Rainey, H. G. (2009). *Understanding and managing public organizations* (4th ed.). Jossey-Bass.

Rainey, H. G. (2014). *Understanding and managing public organizations* (5th ed.). Jossey-Bass.

Rainey, H. G., Backoff, R. W., & Levine, C. H. (1976). Comparing public and private organizations. *Public Administration Review, 36*(2), 233-244.

Robbins, S. P., & Judge, T. A. (2011). *Organizational behavior* (4th ed.). Pearson.

Rothschild, J. (1977). Observation on political legitimacy in contemporary Europe. *Political Science Quarterly, 92,* 874-501.

Ryan, R . M. & Deci, E. L. (2000), Self-determination theory and the facilitation of intrinsic motivation, social development, and well-Being. *American Psychologist, 55*(1): 68~78

Sambrook. S., & Stewart. J. (2007). *Human resource development in health and social care.* Routledge.

Schein, E. H. (1980). *Organization psychology.* Prentice-Hall.

Schein, E. H. (1985). *Organizational culture and leadership.* Jossey-Bass.

Schein, E. H. (1992). *Organizational culture and leadership* (2nd ed.). Jossey-Bass.

Schein, E. H. (1996). Culture: the missing concept in organization studies. *Administrative Science Quarterly, 41,* 229-240.

Schein, E. H. (2004). Organizational culture and leadership (3rd ed.). Sage.

Seibert, S. E., Kraimer, M. L., & Liden, R. C. (2001). A social capital theory of career success. *Academy of Management Journal, 44*(2), 219-237.

Slocum, J. W., & Hellriegel, D. (2011). *Principles of organizational behavior* (13th ed.). South-Western Cengage Learning.

Spear, L. C. (2010). Character and servant leadership: The characteristics of effective, caring leaders. *The Journal of Virtues & Leadership, 1*(1), 25-30.

Stoker, G. (2006). Public value management: A new narrative for networked governance? *American Review of Public Administration, 36*(1), 41-57.

Taylor, F. W. (1914). *The principles of scientific management.* Harper.

Thomas, K. W. Conflict and negotiation processes in organizations. In M. D. Dunnette., & L. M. Kough (Eds.), *Handbook of industrial and organizational psychology* (Vol. 3, 2nd ed.). Consulting Psychologists Press.

Thompson, F. J. (1989). Managing within civil service systems. In J. L. Perry (ed.), *Handbook of public administration*. Jossey-Bass.

Treasury Board of Canada Secretariat. (2000). *Results for canadians: A management framework for the government of canada*.

Treasury Board of Canada Secretariat. (2009a). *Guidelines on the Performance Management Program for Executives 2009-2010*.

Treasury Board of Canada Secretariat. (2009b). *Treasury Board of Canada Secretariat Five-Year Evaluation of the MAF Final Report*.

Vroom, V. (1964). *Work and motivation*. John Wiley & Sons.

Wahyudi, E., & Park, S. M. (2014). Unveiling the value creation process of electronic human resource management: An Indonesian case. *Public Personnel Management*, *43*(1), 83-117.

Wart, M. V. (2003). Public-sector leadership theory: An assessment. *Public Administration Review*, *63*, 214-228.

Werner, J. M., & DeSimone, R. L. (2006). *Human resource development* (4th ed.). Thomson South-Western.

Wood, R., & Bandura, A. (1989). Social cognitive theory of organizational management. *The Academy of Management Review*, 14(3), 361-384.

Word, J., & Park, S. M. (2009). Working across the divide: Job involvement in the public and nonprofit sectors. *Review of Public Personnel Administration*, 29(2), 103-133.

Korea Joonang Daily (2013.05.28)

Pacific Standard (2014.07.01)

Pingdon (2012.01.31)

The Korea Herald (2005.10.25)

The Korea Herald (2014.02.02)

The Korea Herald. (2014.05.19)

The Korea Times (2008.01.24)

The Korea Times (2008.11.24)

The Korea Times (2012.05.28)

The Korea Times (2013.06.05)

The Korea Times (2013.07.11)

Yonhap News Agency (2013.03.25)

Yonhap News Agency (2013.07.02)